LIFE WORK

7

G

DONALD HALL

LIFE WORK

BEACON PRESS · BOSTON

Beacon Press
25 Beacon Street
Boston, Massachusetts 02108-2892

Beacon Press books
are published under the auspices of
the Unitarian Universalist Association of Congregations.

99 98 97 96 95 94 93   8 7 6 5 4 3 2

Text design by Barry Moser
Title-page lettering by Reassurance Wunder
Composition by Wilsted & Taylor Publishing Services

Library of Congress Cataloging-in-Publication Data

Hall, Donald, 1928–
Life work / Donald Hall.

p.   cm.

ISBN 0-8070-7054-8

I. Hall, Donald, 1928–   —Biography. 2. Poets, American—
20th century—Biography. 3. Authorship. 4. Work. I. Title.

PS3515.A3152Z475   1993

811'.54—dc20

[B]   93-18418

CIP

FOR LUCY AT NINETY

WORK IS THE ONLY PRACTICAL CONSOLATION FOR
HAVING BEEN BORN.

—Miguel de Unamuno

CONSIDER THE LILIES OF THE FIELD, HOW THEY
GROW; THEY NEITHER TOIL NOR SPIN.

—Matthew 6:28

ADMIRABLE IS THAT RELIGION OF THE OLD MONKS,
LABORARE EST ORARE, WORK IS WORSHIP.

—Thomas Carlyle

O, WHY DON'T YOU WORK
LIKE OTHER MEN DO?
HOW IN HELL CAN I WORK
WHEN THERE'S NO WORK TO DO?

O, I LIKE MY BOSS—
HE'S A GOOD FRIEND OF MINE;
THAT'S WHY I AM STARVING
OUT IN THE BREADLINE.

—The Little Red Songbook

WE MUST WORK THE WORKS OF HIM WHO SENT ME,
WHILE IT IS DAY: NIGHT COMES, WHEN NO ONE CAN
WORK.

—John 9:4

ONE

I'VE NEVER WORKED A day in my life. With the trivial exceptions of some teenage summers, I've never worked with my hands or shoulders or legs. I never stood on the line in Flint among the clangor and stench of embryonic Buicks for ten hours of small operations repeated on a large machine. Oh, I've watched this work, visiting a plant; I've watched *Modern Times* also. When I taught at the University of Michigan, many of my students worked summers installing gas tanks at River Rouge or building generators in Ypsilanti. Some of them came from families of line-workers; the university was a way out of Flint and Toledo. These children of line-parents moved to desks in offices, nine-to-five, which was my own father's work, and which I escaped. Doubtless my grandfather Hall, my father, and I made a stereotypical three generations: My father's father grew up without much school, doing muscle-work, and built a successful business; so he sent my father to college who worked out his life at a desk adding columns of figures among blonde-wood cubicles where properly dressed men and women worked with numbers five days a week and half a day on Saturday. Then there's me: I stay home and write poems—and essays, stories, textbooks, children's books, biography . . . Work?

Work. I make my living at it. Almost twenty years ago I quit teaching—giving up tenure, health insurance, and annual raises—as one of my children began college and the other was about to. I worked like crazy to pay tuitions and mortgages—but because I loved my work it was as if I did not work at all.

There are jobs, there are chores, and there is work. Reading proof is a chore; checking facts is a chore. When I edit for a magazine or a publisher, I do a job. When I taught school, the classroom fit none of these categories. I enjoyed teaching James Joyce and Thomas Wyatt too much to call it a job. The classroom was a lark because I got to show off, to read poems aloud, to help the young, and to praise authors or books that I loved. But teaching was not entirely larkish: Correcting piles of papers is tedious, even discouraging, because it tends to correct one's sanguine notions about having altered the young minds arranged in the classroom's rows. Reading papers was a chore—and after every ten papers, I might tell myself that I could take a break and read a Flannery O'Connor short story. But when I completed the whole pile, then I could reward myself with a real break: When I finished reading and correcting and grading and commenting on seventy-five essay-questions about a Ben Jonson or a Tom Clark poem, *then*—as a reward—I could get to work.

From the middle sixties into the seventies I saw Dr. M. M. Frolich in Ann Arbor, which at that time supported more psychoanalysts than Vienna. My first marriage was thrashing itself to death, I was unhappy—and it was the thing to do. Dr. Frolich, the only local analyst who did therapy, helped me greatly—as I saw him once a week when things were tepid, three times a week when the psyche hotted up. He didn't help by talking but by raising his eyebrows when I talked. Over the years I learned how to be helped: When I walked into his office I started emptying my mind out, thoughts of the instant, not thoughts saved to tell my therapist. I learned to be unguarded enough to allow slips of the tongue, always grist for the mill. Once in a headlong sentence I clearly intended to say "life" but by mistake (as the actress said to the bishop) said "work" instead. Dr. Frolich's gentle gray head nodded in confirmation.

Today I begin *Life Work*. We were up at four-fifteen this morning, and at six we drove to New London for a small ceremony: Jack Jensen died two years ago today (St. Patrick's Day) and Jane organized a memorial at the marble bench erected in Jack's memory outside his office at Colby-Sawyer College where he taught philosophy. I worked on a poem before we drove the twelve miles to stand in a circle, six of us, reading Scripture and praying. I was as cold as I have ever been; it occurred to me, in my egotism, that my suffering was appropriate to the anniversary. Do I think I will suffer Jack out of purgatory? Jack's own theology mocks me. He was our minister, with a degree in philosophy to go with his divinity degree; often he was more philosophical than mystical and he never spoke of purgatory. Jane and I loved him, and his death two years ago was devastation.

We moved to New Hampshire in 1975, to undertake the life of free-lance writing, and to live in the farmhouse my great-grandparents bought in 1865. My grandmother was born here in 1878 and my mother in 1903. Our first Sunday in New Hampshire I thought: "*They* will expect us to go to church." I suppose *they* were my cousins; church was the small white clapboard South Danbury Christian Church two miles north, which my great-grandparents Ben and Lucy Keneston helped to build in 1868, and where my grand-mother played the organ seventy-eight years, from the age of fourteen until she was ninety-two, and where I sat on Sun-days as a child when I visited my grandparents. For decades I had not gone to church, nor had Jane, and we went that first Sunday grudgingly, without enthusiasm, to hear the young man in the pulpit quote "the German poet Rilke"—which pricked up our poetical ears.

But there was something else, something that endures—a community radiating the willingness or even the desire to be careful and loving. This community was my cousin Edna, her sister Martha, our cousin Audrey, Annie Walker who played the organ following my grandmother, and other neighbors who assumed us into their rows as if we had just returned from a journey. The tender welcome was irresist-ible, and we went again the next Sunday and the next. One Sunday morning Jane was ill and stayed in bed; I would stay home with her—but five minutes before Church I knew I had to go, and sped off in the Plymouth, astonished at my desire.

In the meantime Jack's sermons touched us: Jane was first to follow him; I followed Jane as we read Scripture and then saints and mystics. I found Meister Eckhart and Jane Julian of Norwich as well as Saint Teresa—do our hormones choose our metaphysicians?—as we joined a two thousand year history, full of murder and compassion and grace, under Jack Jensen's leadership. We saw him sometimes for dinner or at a party, saw him drink too much and argue—with me to aid and abet. We learned how he lived, how hard he worked. At Colby-Sawyer he taught philosophy and the his-tory of religions, five classes sometimes, and taught every day arousing the sometimes-lethargic young women of his small college. Also he counseled them, formally and informally, all the while he ministered to us. For years he worked on a long novel out of the classical world—he admired Yourcenar's great *Memoirs of Hadrian*; he admired Mary Renault; most of all he loved the classical world, and visiting Greece was overwhelmed to walk in the Athenian agora where Paul and Plato walked—but he was not a novelist. He was a minister; on Saturday afternoons, for most of his life, he wrote his sermons. We heard him when he was spiritually alert and lively, and heard him when he was exiled and thirsty in the desert. When skepticism rode him as a jockey rides a horse, his sermons were historical and philosophical, dry but informative; but then the rains would come, especially during Advent when he waited again for the birth, or in contemplating personal saints like Dietrich Bonhoffer. The Christian year enthralled us, and rhymed with the countryside's year: the birth in cold and snow, Maundy Thursday with its journey toward torture and death, Easter with its sunburst of resurrection. Jack permitted me to alternate skepticism with Christianity. When Jane and I visited China in 1986, reading our poems for USIS, on Easter we went to a Chinese church, two bignoses among five hundred enduring Chinese Protestants, and when I heard the choir belt out, in Chinese, "Up from the grave He arose," I felt myself melted into two millennia of the round world.

Then Jack discovered a problem in his abdomen. Doctors could not agree whether it was cancer or not, an ambiguous cell structure, but they tried chemo just in case. He returned to health but later the symptoms returned; more chemo, which had to cease because it destroyed red blood cells. Jane and I were in Boston, baby-sitting a friend and his small daughter while her mother was hospitalized for a minor operation, when the phone rang: Jack had two days to live. So we sat by his bedside as he turned cold. The last night, Jane and another friend spent the darkness beside him as his breaths grew slower, repeating,

> Lord, have mercy upon us.
> Christ, have mercy upon us.
> Lord, have mercy upon us.

At six-thirty the next morning, exhausted, with Jack unresponsive, Jane drove home to sleep. I held Jack's cold hand in her stead. I was fetching a cup of coffee when Jack died early on the morning of March 17, two years ago today.

Today we threw tuberoses—Jane bought them in Cambridge yesterday—onto the granite bench and drove home, where I returned to my poem and an essay almost finished and a letter recommending a poet to a prize panel. Meantime, Jane in her study upstairs worked on her own poems. After an hour, I was ready to begin *Life Work*. Every day I will write a few pages on the subject. I will write about my own work and the sensibilities I derive from, my parents and my grandparents. Oh, I have many notions about work. I *would*: Whatever I write about—when I write an essay or a children's book, when I write about the ox-cart man or Dock Ellis or Henry Moore; when I try putting everything I know into a poem—always I write about *work*. When I talked with Dylan Thomas in my early twenties I asked how he worked; now if I meet a twenty-three year old with talent, I determine how she works.

That's enough for today. Work is my obsession but it is also my devotion. Jack Jensen loved to work and it was one of the bonds between us. Work is not redemptive—God's work—but it is or it can be devoted.

☙

My Connecticut father's father was Henry Hall, who married Augusta Wuestefeld, whose father Andreas was a cabinetmaker and emigrant from Hanover (the family had lived in a house, I was told, where the poet Heine had lived) to Orange Street in New Haven. I have a children's toybox he knocked together for my father. The five children of Dorothea and Andreas knew no idle hours: Work was holy; work was the daily text of the life lived. For recreation the brothers and sisters Wuestefeld played bridge and teased each other heavily. My grandmother Augusta was witty, seeing through all surfaces to the greedy bone. When she was a young wife—with Henry Hall's dairy business thriving—she handled the books with a shrewd, exact, and scrupulous eye.

My great-grandfather Charlie Hall, Henry's father, worked hard but played harder. A working man, he labored building New Haven's reservoir (off Armory Street in Hamden) in 1860, with a wife and two children at home in a cottage near the icehouses by Lake Whitney, and one day at noon walked off the job without telling his boss or his wife, walked four miles to the Green in New Haven and enlisted for a year in the war for Union, the war against slaveowners and rebels. I preserve the combination knife-fork-spoon he ate with, fighting in the West, and the bugle he blew. After his one year he came home, taking no pleasure in the work of war; later when he was drafted he bought a substitute rather than fight—even though as a laborer he needed to borrow the money.

This purchase never impeded his later expressions of patriotism, as on the Fourth of July through the eighties and nineties he led Charlie Hall's Fife and Drum Corps in Hamden parades. Maybe nothing much bothered him. Rumors suggest he took pleasure in alcohol. When he died of a stroke, not young, family stories tell that his widow stood by the head of his coffin, weeping, as two strange women glared at each other across the foot.

Sometimes I make lists of things to do in years ahead: a prose book I mean to write; a new book of poems, with a guess at the year when it ought to finish itself; new short stories; revision of a textbook. These lists get lost. Opening an old notebook, I find a list from the late 1970s. It surprises me to find that I had already planned something accomplished a decade later; it surprises me that I wrote so many things I planned to write. But also, I notice a forgotten project that interests me again: In the old notebook I make new notes.

Monthly lists take a place beside my blue living-room chair; on my desk, I keep a list of ongoing things—like *Life Work*—and smaller projects that will take three or four weeks: reviewing Tom Williams's short stories for the *Globe*; doing a piece on graveyards for *Harrowsmith*; outlining a proposal for a children's book. When a project turns active with drafts and revisions, I put a checkmark beside it to identify it as ongoing—as if I needed to inform myself. Apparently I like to make checkmarks. Like all listmakers, I enjoy drawing lines through items that I have finished. Listmakers without exception occasionally accomplish some task which they never planned to do, and which they never put on a list;

listmakers write the item down, in order to feel the satisfaction of crossing it out.

When the *Britannica* takes on Work, it qualifies the noun and addresses "Work, Organization of," but it supplies a definition when you're not looking: Work is "activities necessary to society's survival." (The *Britannica* does not think of work as something people *do*; everything is passive.) How boring it sounds, like most discussions of work. When Adam Smith talks about the eighteen divisions of labor in making a pin, or when Emile Durkheim does something similar, I fall asleep. Slaveowner Cicero writes more to my taste.

It is the family farm—which historians of work's structure derive from utter antiquity—that provides a model for my own work; one task after another, all day all year, and every task different. Of course: It was precisely the Connecticut family business of the Brock-Hall Dairy—milk pasteurizing and bottling and delivering; every-day-the-same, temporarily efficient subdivision of the industrial world; my father's curse—that I grew up determined to avoid or evade. And did.

In the "Day-Timer" beside my blue chair I keep a daily list. It is a pleasure, sleepy at night watching the Red Sox one-run behind in the seventh inning, to pick up the "Day-Timer," tear off today's corner, flip to tomorrow's page and list the next day's work. Recent pages read "Mertens at 2" (an interview about the National Endowment for the Arts); "5 o'clock Jerry" (my appointment with the dentist who is my son-in-law); and "Ct" (driving to Connecticut for a visit with my mother.) Most days begin with laconic single words in a semantic order:

11

> poems
> prose

but today I write "proses" to suggest multiplicity: the tenth or eighteenth version of a periodical piece as well as a letter of recommendation and a proposal to the New Hampshire Arts Council. Underneath "proses" I place another pair of syllables:

Life Work

Doubtless italic permits me to distinguish general from particular, and late in the day I will draw a straight line through:

> ~~poems~~
> ~~proses~~
> ~~*Life Work*~~

and a wavery line, to indicate failure, through the projects I didn't get to, as it were:

My Connecticut great-grandfather Charlie Hall worked with his hands. After the reservoir job and the war, as an older man with a grown family, he worked for Farmer Webb in a part of Hamden now called, after a 1920 developer's dainty device of onomastic invention, Spring Glen. Charlie was a farmhand when my grandfather Henry (1875–1966) was born in a worker's cottage belonging to Farmer Webb. One of Charlie's tasks, in middle age, was to milk Webb's cattle and deliver raw milk from the pail into the receptacles of Webb's cowless neighbors. When Charlie quarreled with his boss, as the family story records, he started his own business by buying milk from another farmer to sell to Webb's customers. From hired hand he became middleman, founding the Hall Dairy—that would grow, expand, combine with Charlie Brock's to become Brock-Hall Dairy, wax over southern Connecticut, acquire moribund family dairies, metamorphose stables of workhorses into fleets of delivery trucks . . . and finally fail, *fail*, as supermarkets with loss-leader half-gallon milk cartons knocked out home delivery in the 1950s and 1960s.

My grandfather Henry Hall labored for Farmer Webb as a boy, odd jobs a boy could do, especially in harvest. When he was ninety years old, he lived on Norris Street in a suburban block of Spring Glen built over Farmer Webb's strawberry fields, where as a boy he had picked strawberries for ten cents an hour. At ninety, he told such stories in a deep slow voice, shaking his head over the changes he had lived to see—bewildered by progress, still commanding, never judging the effects of change.

Henry quit school about 1885, after the fifth grade, and worked beside his father. When Charlie Hall quarreled with Webb and went off on his own, Henry worked with his father. They built up two routes for the home delivery of milk, invested in glass to deliver milk in bottles—O luxury of innovation!—which they washed by hand every day in

13

the kitchen of a rented house. People moved out to Hamden from New Haven, especially to Whitneyville, two miles closer to the city than Spring Glen. Maybe the trolley came as far out as Whitneyville, allowing workers to commute. Before Charlie died, he and Henry disputed over expansion. Charlie believed in keeping small, his son in expanding.

Henry Hall expanded. When I first remember the Brock-Hall Dairy, in the early 1930s, we (I relished the pronoun) built a big milk processing plant on Whitney Avenue in Whitneyville. (Eli Whitney had built workers' housing in the nineteenth century—Whitney's Village—when he raised a gun factory beside the dam at the end of the lake.) Who built a plant in 1934? Home delivery of good milk prospered—the cream line on *our* Grade A was deeper than any other dairy's—and route added to route, and behind the new brick building stretched long low wooden stables for the fifty great shaggy workhorses that pulled the red wagons of Brock-Hall.

Henry expanded, Henry prospered, and Henry knew exactly how he did it. He was a man of few words but, like E. B. White's William Strunk, he said his words three times: "Woik-woik-woik," I heard him say in his eighties—retired from management, working long days in his garden and as volunteer caretaker in the Whitneyville Cemetery where Augusta lay. The southern New Englander's old-fashioned accent pronounced vowels as Brooklyn did. (Walt Whitman's accent, who said "pome" not "poem," must have resembled Henry Hall's.) "Keep your health," he said in one of his longer sentences, "keep your health—and woik-woik-woik."

Henry passed to his grandson, as he approached and passed ninety, the secret of life.

My New Hampshire grandmother Kate's mother, Lucy Buck Keneston, died young at sixty, and the narrative of her illness describes a burst appendix and peritonitis. Lucy Buck's mother Nancy—married to a coachman in Andover—had been known as the best of spinners, and daughter followed mother: Lucy's own spinning wheel for sheep's wool tilts in our attic now. In this house where nothing was ever discarded some old braided rugs must include products of Nancy's and Lucy's spinning.

Lucy's husband Ben Keneston was my maternal great-grandfather, born in John Quincy Adams's presidency and dead in Woodrow Wilson's. Although he died fifteen years before I was born, I speak of him as if I knew him; this house is full of him. He bought the Cape, built onto it, and settled here in 1865—where my grandmother was born thirteen years later. She was the baby and the favorite and never stopped talking about him, even when she was old. Ben was born in Andover, half a mile from coachman Buck, where his Keniston grandfather (Ben changed the spelling) had migrated north from Cambridge after fighting in the Revolution. The first Keniston of Andover lies in the old cemetery. When he was young Ben bought land high on the north end of Ragged Mountain and raised sheep. In our storage place which we call the back chamber there is an old box of wool with a legend in a fragile hand: "Wool was from B. C. Keniston's sheep carded at Otterville 1848." I figure he saved it because it was his first crop.

When Ben Keneston accumulated any money, he put it into land: no cash, many acres. After he made money selling wool during the war, he bought this house—beside the

Grafton Turnpike and the railroad line in a narrow valley west of Ragged Mountain halfway between Danbury and Andover. For his growing family he added rooms, extending it back into the foot of Ragged with a toolshed, a milkroom, a woodshed, and an outhouse. Detached and up hill because of the hazard of fire, his great barn rises where he kept his cows, horses, oxen, and pigs; the barn stands as the house does. Across the narrow turnpike he built the sheepbarn, with open sheds alongside to shelter hayrack and rake, and next to the sheds the henyard. In the months they went without pasture, fences penned the sheep where sheds and barn stopped. Fronting the Grafton Turnpike Ben Keneston made a watering trough, fence running over the middle of it: Sheep could drink from the barnyard side, turnpike-traveling teams from the other.

The cowbarn lay along Ragged's incline, the west side dropping down, manure pile underneath tie-up and pigpen beside manure pile. The east wall underneath the barn is huge slabs of granite wedged against Ragged's earth.

John Wells, my New Hampshire grandfather Wesley's father, was a blacksmith who fought in the Civil War, all four years unlike his Connecticut counterpart Charlie Hall. John Wells never talked about the war, which frustrated my grandfather when he could not answer my questions about his father's soldiering. I call John Wells a blacksmith, which he was, but like everyone in the country his work was a thousand things. Every man outside the city was a farmer—be he lawyer, minister, doctor, or blacksmith—because without refrigeration (except for the icebox, using transparent blocks sawed from the winter ponds and preserved in sawdust)

every family kept a cow, and keeping a cow fresh meant a heifer every year or two and meant borrowing or hiring the services of a bull; it meant haying in summer. And every family kept chickens for eggs. And every family grew a huge garden and canned vegetables and fruit, the woodstove burning red in hottest summer with kettles of blueberries or tomatoes; and the root cellar filled with apples, potatoes, squash, beets, carrots, and cabbages.

Someone like John Wells blacksmithed for cash, shoeing the neighborhood horses and repairing or forging ironware, hinges, and tools. Doubtless he tapped trees to make maple syrup and sugar; certainly he kept bees for honey. The house where he lived, where my grandfather Wesley grew up, stands only two and a half miles from this house, handsome and solitary and still cared for. I love to imagine the Wellses there a century ago. Once a year when the trout stream behind his house ran fast with end-of-winter melt, John Wells used water power to saw up boards enough to build one carriage, and blacksmith turned wheelwright. He didn't require storing much ice, because he didn't sell milk to H. P. Hood as the cow-farmers did. He required timber not only for the carriage but for the cookstove's heat and for the twenty-four-hour fire that turned maplesap to syrup and sugar. Also, on clear nights when the moon was full, John Wells chopped firewood for his neighbor at a dollar a cord, stacked and ready for transport. Until I heard this story I never understood how "moonlighting" meant what it meant.

He was frugal. His wife Martha made cakes without vanilla—maple or honey gave flavor—because a bottle of vanilla cost cash money. Did he work on the road to pay his town taxes? Many did, carting hardpan to fill a washout, repairing bridges, rolling the road after snowstorms so that sleighs could slide over packed snow. When he received his veteran's pension he would not spend it; it went into a savings account, and before he died he gave each of his seven children a thousand dollars.

It is evident, in the accent of New Hampshire, that "John Wells never was afraid of wuk." Woik for Connecticut, wuk for New Hampshire. Among my four sets of great-grandparents—Hall, Wuestefeld, Keneston, Wells; two Civil War veterans, two farmers, one farmhand, one cabinet-maker; three Yankees and one German—there was little in common except a proclivity for hard work.

My old OED goes thirty columns from Work the noun ("Something that is or was done"—first citation 977 A.D.) through the verb and its use in phrases—Work out, Work up—before it reaches Workability. The OED's Supplement offers almost nine columns more, mostly discoveries of other early citations. The first use of Workaholic—"One who is addicted to work, or who voluntarily works excessively hard and unusually long hours"—is attributed to W. E. Oates, *Pastoral Psychology*, 16 October 1968. Question for 1993, true or false: "All great-grandparents were workaholics." Oh, the 1968 coinage merely measures our distance from 1868. When the OED Supplement defines its new word, it cites: "The workaholic, as an addict is called, neglects his family, withdraws from social life, and loses interest in sex." John Wells for one will not qualify. There were seven children; his work was at home, the blacksmith's shop attached to the barn that attached to the house. Seven children and two adults worked together every day, never neglecting each other not because of moral resolve but because they could not avoid each other.

Nor did the family avoid public things: John Wells lived in service to a consuming passion—which was the politics of the Democratic Party. Or was his great passion loathing Re-

18

publicans? His distaste for Republicans began with Lincoln and included his neighbors, for then as now New Hampshire was a Republican domain. Not that he loathed his neighborhood in general, only its politics: This Copperhead fought in the Civil War—Company F, 15th Regiment, New Hampshire Volunteers—out of loyalty to his bailiwick. Apparently the Wells's dinner table, every noon, was as loud with argument as a national convention. Although the men were all Democrats, they agreed about nothing except the probity and intelligence of the Republican party.

My mother was twenty when her grandfather John died. She knew him as an old veteran, proud and intensely political. When he died she was old enough to vote, and even allowed to—as her mother was not, until she was fifty years old. Today I receive a letter from my mother Lucy in Connecticut, eighty-nine years old a month from today in the house we moved to in 1936. The letter tells me that she made chicken soup the day before, and froze ten portions. Making chicken soup is not a trivial accomplishment on the corner of Ardmore and Greenway in 1992. Lucy's mind is fine but her body is painful; arthritis hobbles her; spinal stenosis bends her over and makes it difficult for her to walk to the kitchen or the toilet, her two destinations. She cooks for herself— and for us when we visit once a month to gossip and do errands—in five-minute bursts. She must sit back in her recliner, after five minutes, for pain to recede and breath to return. For herself, she freezes meatloaf slices, portions of chicken, tripe. Yesterday—she writes me—she also finished two aprons, which she makes as presents or for the fancywork table at our South Danbury Church Fair. She tells me she's almost done reading the large-type Amy Tan we brought her last month. Day before yesterday, she tells me,

she wrote *five* letters, and maybe tomorrow she'll answer the
other four that she still owes . . .

❦

Each morning now, working on poetry before I get to *Life
Work*, I redraft "Another Elegy." It takes me many drafts to
write a poem and "Another Elegy" is the all-time statistical
leader. When I take questions after a poetry reading, or talk
to student poets, I emphasize how hard I work and how many
drafts I number. (A few weeks ago I talked in Chicago. My
host in a recent letter quoted a student: "I was amazed about
his overdrafts.") Seldom do I mention "Another Elegy," because its numbers are ridiculous. Some poems get finished,
over a year or two, in twenty-five or thirty drafts; more likely
fifty or sixty; several by actual count go over a hundred—but
"Another Elegy," which began in 1982, had accumulated—
when I put it away in 1988, furious with it, ashamed and hu-
miliated by failure—over five hundred drafts. At some point
in 1990 this poem began to nibble at my consciousness again.
I had put it away but I hadn't destroyed it, and I began to consider a fundamental alteration in the way the poem presented
itself. For a year I refused its entreaties, would not look at it;
then on January 1, 1992, with the deepest of sighs, I pulled it
out of the drawer. It looked good to me, and immediately I
began radical revision; deep hopelessness seesawed to eleva-
tions of high hope. After ten more weeks and thirty more
drafts I showed the new poem to Jane who remembered the
old one; her response encouraged me.

Always I hope that I might be doing my Best Work, although I understand that it is unlikely at sixty-three and a
half. I work on "Another Elegy," manic, first thing in the
day; or I work on it *all* day, because if I drive to my daugh-

ter's in Concord I stop by the road and take notes. I start waking at two or three in the morning, putting on my glasses to see the clock because I want to wake and get back to this poem. (But if I get up before four-thirty I ruin my day with early fatigue.) When the coffee grinds itself at quarter to five, I am out of bed in one second.

And all the time, part of my mind keeps reminding me: "You felt like this, about this same poem, a hundred times between 1982 and 1988."

In 1975 when we first moved here my cousin Paul Fenton told me a story that I made into a poem and a children's book. Now I tell the story again to make a point. Paul the storyteller was a farmer, a good Democrat who accepted federal preferment when the Democrats were in power, a UNH graduate, a teacher and educational administrator—and he resembled his uncle, my grandfather Wesley, especially when he remembered a story and the skin crimped around his eyes. "Did you ever hear the one," said Paul as he sat on our sofa, "about the fellow—used to live around here—who filled up his ox-cart every year with everything his family made or grew that was left over? Maple sugar I suppose, wool and woolens, maybe linen or flaxseed, shingles, birch brooms, potatoes. Every year he filled his cart and walked by his ox to Portsmouth Market—once he went all the way to Boston— and sold everything out of his cart. Then he sold his cart. Then he sold his ox." This was the climax and surprise of the story; when Paul saw my happy response, he grinned again. "Then he walked home and started getting next year's ox ready, building a new ox-cart I guess . . ."

Stories like these hover in the air for generations, waiting

21

for some bat-writer to swoop down and gobble them. Paul said an old man had told him the story when he was a boy; and Paul said that the old man said that when *he* was a boy, an *old* man had told it to him. So I took the story, with Paul's permission, and told it in print as a poem, and as a children's book which must have sold a million copies by now. It's a tale of work-work-work, of total dispersal and starting again, of human life compared to a perennial plant that dies to rise again.

But the point I want to make about my story concerns attitudes to work. When I had finished the poem-version, published it in the *New Yorker*, and read it from the platform, I discovered that responses to the poem divided people. Half felt the exhilaration I felt in the ox-cart man's work-cycle; another half found the story discouraging, all that work and you have to do it over again. Temperament, temperament. Each human division reads the same story; each responds from an opposite place.

November of 1991 Jane and I spent three weeks careering through India talking for USIS. USIS worked us hard: We lectured and gave readings in the morning and late afternoon. At breakfast we were interviewed for newspapers, Jane as early as six o'clock one morning. These interviews were often our own doing not USIS's: At a reading a young anxious charming Indian would tell us that his newspaper wanted a piece; we would add another interview at 7:30 A.M. In the evenings there were dinner parties with literary and artistic people, beginning with drinks at eight, supper served at ten o'clock. Usually we could nap after lunch.

At dinner parties we met poets, playwrights, actors, academics, and film people. One leading poet was a bank president, another a doctor. One night I had a long conversation with a novelist named Gurcharan Das who is CEO for Procter and Gamble in India; we compared notes on Cincinnati, where I lectured on poetry twenty-five years before, and which he visits quarterly on Procter and Gamble business. He told me a story in order to bring up a subject. A week earlier, he had addressed a conference in Bombay which gathered four hundred young Indian managers for instruction in the ways of business. In the question period one young man raised his hand to ask, "What is contentment?"

The novelist-CEO told me the story because he wanted to talk about contentment. I tell it first—with pleasure in India—as a story about the country: Indians don't small-talk; they Introduce Topics. (When I met P. Lal, poet and translator, he looked me in the eye and said, "What you think of irony?") For me, the lesson I learned from Gurcharan Das was not so much the nature of contentment as the nature of Indian managers. If an American junior executive asked such a question in public, would he remain a junior executive?

The moment Das repeated the question I knew my answer: Contentment is work so engrossing that you do not know that you are working. I asked him what he answered, and he told me: "I said, 'Give me two minutes and I will answer your question.' I took two minutes while they waited. Then I told them that contentment was *absorbedness*." So Gurcharan Das's answer and mine were the same. I liked his word; a noun with a lot of verb in it. ("Absorption" sounds too much like paper towels.) With enthusiasm I agreed with him, speaking of early morning hours, concentration on the page and its words, total loss of identity, hours that pass like seconds or without any notion of time elapsing: It is always the *paradox* of contentment—of happiness or joy—that to remain at its pitch it must include no consciousness of itself; you are only content when you have no notion of contentment.

Yes, Gurcharan Das answered my question, sometimes he felt this absorbedness in his business, yes . . . but not so much as in writing fiction. His latest novel, *A Fine Family*, had started slowly, they all do, but then it livened itself, and his writing time (weekends; snatched hours waiting for India Air in the Delhi Airport; half an hour before dawn on a weekday) rose to the highest pitch.

"Only making love," I said, "is anything like it." His head bobbed in agreement; he grinned with conspiracy.

Today makes a week of *Life Work*. As I walk the dog, or watch spring training games from Florida while struggling to finish my income tax, I think about work and take notes. Driving I keep a little tape machine beside me. I am *absorbed*, in this book and in "Another Elegy." Every day I have ideas for poem and essay, and every day make another draft of the poem and add pages of this prose to the *Life Work* pile. Do I fiddle too much with the poem as I approach six hundred bloody drafts? Do I repeat the same tone and feeling in all my work-anecdotes? I am swept away: I am happy; I am manic. Am I manic? Who else counts the numbers of drafts? Like Wade Boggs I know not only how many singles I have hit but also what count I had each single on, where it went, and what kind of pitch I hit. (I know even more detail about striking out with the bases loaded.) But I know none of these things while I am writing at the desk. I am utterly happy, utterly unself-conscious.

Then I remember—sagging suddenly, heavy as mud, black, and hopeless—all the times I have felt this way, writing poems especially but occasionally essays, when I have come later to realize that the words I wrote with such excitement were nothing, nothing, nothing at all, and my excitement (my certainty!) merely a function of blood chemistry. One disease of working alone—the way writers mostly work—is dependence on mood. Mood is no measure and flips from highest to lowest in a millisecond.

Feeling miserable over work that fails is preferable to depression which makes work impossible. When I feel overwhelmed by too many things to do, or frustrated by my inability to sustain work over a twenty-four hour day, or unable to keep up with the ideas that rattle in my skull, I suspend discontent by remembering months and years of anguish and lethargy, lying on twisted sheets, painful, too miserable to get out of bed. *Oblomov* is the textbook, the man who cannot get out of bed. What's to get up for? Writers are bipolar by nature and by nature extreme. In the years between marriages I remained *low*, playing at *high*, through years that were twelve months of winter, blue frost all day all month all year. Thinking of my death was thinking of paradise or at least respite from pain. Self-medication by alcohol gave temporary relief, brief lethal holiday and foretaste of death. (Work, as Oscar Wilde reminds us, is the curse of the drinking classes.) Now if I complain of superabundance I must remember: *Too much* is so far happier than *too little* that they do not belong on the same seesaw.

Absorbedness is the paradise of work, but what is its provenance or etiology? Surely it is an ecstasy of transport, of loss of ego; but it is also something less transcendent: To work is to please the powerful masters who are parents—who are family, who are church, who are custom or culture. Not to work is to violate the contract or to disobey the injunction, and to displease the dispensers of supper and love, of praise's reward. Not working becomes conviction of unworthiness. We prove ourselves worthy by the numbers of work.

When I sold lightbulbs door-to-door for the Andover Lions Club, every October a woman in Danbury told me about how much she had canned that year. She lived in a small rickety cottage, almost a shack, with an old propane cooker. Each year her prodigies increased in prodigiousness. She told me: "This year I did 347 peas, 414 string beans, 77 peaches, 402 corn, 150 strawberry jams . . ." She talked plain, the New Hampshire way without affect, but I felt pride surging in every century of Ball jars, self-worth assembled in dense rows of vegetable love packed into her root cellar. And as I listened I thrilled with her, felt pride with her and for her. Four hundred cans of corn! Did her family *eat* four cans of corn each day all winter? Heavens, no. Every time I visited, I took home several examples of her canning.

Once when I was a teacher I took part in a television panel on English composition in California with two other college professors and a high school teacher. We talked about what each of us wanted from our students and how each of us went about the task; we talked about getting through to students by individual conferences and by comments on their papers. After a while the high school teacher—she was a large vigorous forthright forty-year-old—asked some questions: How many students were we speaking of? How many papers did we correct and hand back every week? One of the professors said eighteen, another twenty-two; I handled about twenty papers a week, teaching one section of comp at the University of Michigan. We had an inkling of the point she was making, and one of us asked the question

26

we were asked to ask. "Three hundred and twenty," she answered.

How I admired her, as she sat with the three pampered males and assured us that she *read* every one and *wrote a comment* on every one and *what's more spoke with each student* at least once a term. I could tell—talking with her before she produced her numbers on camera—that she had the energy and compassion of a wonderful teacher. She must have foregone sleep and stayed up late with high school prose seven nights a week the whole school year. She must have been born with that energy, and she took suitably massive pride in what she did—but what terrible sins and shortcomings did her labors expiate?

As I like to say: I average four books a year—counting revised editions of old books; counting everything I can damned well count. Counting books, book reviews, notes, poems, and essays, I reckon I publish about one item a week, year-in year-out. Were I fifteen years old, this would be the moment when I would pretend to blow on the backs of my fingernails, then rub them against my chest.

Work, work, work.

In 1975 when Jane and I left Ann Arbor, and I quit the university for the free-lance life, Wendell Berry wrote, "Don, don't put in too many acres at once." "Don't worry about a thing," I told Wendell. We know each other better now.

Wendell farms in Kentucky, teaches a little at the university, travels widely lecturing and investigating agricultural practices—and writes superb stories, poems, and essays. As they say, "I don't know how he does it"; but, also, I don't *want* to do it—except for the "superb stories, poems, and essays." Farming with my grandfather Wesley Wells, when I was a boy, was enough farming for me. I loved his company and enjoyed pitching hay or raking-after as long as he stood above me loading the hayrack and remembering stories. It wasn't my own work that seized me but his work and his stories.

When I emulate his habits, I can take storytelling literally; but I must go metaphoric about mucking out the tie-up, and substitute my crossing-out of failed language for his disposal of bovine feces. When Wendell wrote his letter, I already knew that I would put in no acres. Although I would love to keep a horse for riding, I would resent caring for the horse; I knew enough not to keep a horse I resented. At first I put in a big garden, but woodchucks and raccoons and insects ate it up. When I was a boy I could sit on the watering trough across Route 4 an hour at a time, at dawn and dusk, to shoot woodchucks feeding on our beans or peas, but now I was too impatient for such sitting; now I wanted instead to read a book or write one. (I wanted to work.) Each year the big garden grew smaller and Jane— who grew flowers by choice, not corn or stringbeans— worked at the vegetables more than I did. Each winter I dreamed crops, dreamed marvels of canning (I canned some green tomato chutney; I froze some tomatoes and Kentucky Wonders) and each summer I largely failed. Shamefaced I planted no garden at all. Guilty I confessed to Wendell— "I've never worked a day in my life"—who in his kindness granted me absolution: My task, he told me, was to tell the tales of the tribe.

❦

My twenty-fifth college reunion came at the end of our first year here, after I quit my teaching job. I love reunions. I met again the old fellows I had drunk beer with at Cronin's, Master Shallow especially: smooth faces as wrinkled as bark, over pot bellies replacing athletic waists, hair gone or at least its pigment. Most of the classmates I read about in the papers—scientists, professors, writers—stayed away; Harvard's major products turned up: brokers, bankers, businessmen, and lawyers, alumni who matter to the institution because their charitable wealth keeps the institution rich. My old classmates and I chatted and compared notes; one defiant fellow had become a butcher; others spoke of the pleasures of early retirement. In response to a repeated question I told how I had left the university for the family farm where I wrote for a living. A hundred conversations contained the same exclamation, when I made my habits known: The Class of 1951 collectively cried: "What self-discipline!"

In vain did I protest. For me, I told them, it required no discipline to spend my days writing poems and making books. If I loved chocolate to distraction, I said, would you call me self-disciplined for eating a pound of Hershey's Kisses before breakfast? The unvarying frequency of the accusation—that I took the whip to myself every day, while handcuffed to the desk; that my Muse was Miss Whippe-Lash of the Soho storefront, "Discipline Inflicted Wearing Gym Costume"—upset me because the stereotype suggested a melancholy provenance: Did *all* my classmates hate their work so much?

I doubt it. It is conventional to complain about work, and complaining is usually bragging. Our ancestors emigrated to this country, for the most part, to better their material conditions; in the United States it is only acceptable to do something if you claim to do it for money. It is not respectable to work because you love to work.

My grandfather Wesley Wells, son of the blacksmith John, didn't start out to be a farmer. He had little secondary school; he went briefly to Tilton Academy, about twenty miles away, after his one-room school—maybe for a month?—and came home again. He couldn't stand being so far from home and family, a trait of character common to his brothers and their children my cousins. The people who stayed home in the countryside—while others left for Massachusetts and Ohio and California, for the cities and the suburbs, for better-paying work—were not merely the feckless ones, the lazy or the stupid. They were the people for whom place and family came before everything else, not as ideas or ethics but as necessities of feeling. Their genes inhabit my cousins who live where they were born.

When Wesley Wells married my grandmother, it was agreed that he farm with his father-in-law. Benjamin Cilley Keneston lacked a son to take over the prosperous farm; the only son was Luther the minister, never sturdy or strong (which must be why he died so young at eighty-eight). As Kate's husband, Wesley farmed in a son's place.

Before marrying, Wesley had been a storekeeper in Andover and Potter Place, managing for an owner. Gregarious by nature, he enjoyed working in these stores that sold everything: barrels of staples like sugar and flour, bulk raisins and coffee, yard goods and nails. He loved sitting with drummers after work on the porch of the Hotel Potter, smoking a cigar and listening to stories the salesmen told. Every day's work was dense with incident and talk, so different from the decades of largely solitary farming that lay ahead of him. Recently Maurice Pinard told me a story remembered by his Uncle John, who died thirty years ago in the VA hospital up to Lebanon. When John was a boy in the 1890s he lived on Kearsarge, a remote homestead, but from time to time he visited the village of Potter Place, which seemed a metropolis with its two inns, two stores, railway depot, fishmonger's, butcher's, and livery stable. Some twelve-year-old Potter Place gangsters bullied the ten-year-old stranger—Uncle John told young Maurice in the 1930s—and John expected a thrashing until the tall young storekeeper picked up a horsewhip from a bucket full of whips on sale, and approached the group, which scattered. John doubted that Wesley would have *used* the horsewhip.

Earlier, Wesley worked in the hameshop in Andover, his first job away from home. Hames are the wooden frames of horsecollars, preferably made of ash. Wesley worked there less than a year, quitting because breathing fine sawdust all day made him cough all night. When he told me about the hameshop, fifty years later, he sounded as if he enjoyed the factory work; but it was his temperament to enjoy things. The work week was six days, 6:00 A.M. to 6:00 P.M., and apparently the farmboys who worked there could hardly believe their good fortune: no work on Sunday, and only twelve hours on weekdays! Around 1900 the bosses, overcome by benignity, cut Saturday afternoons so that the shop's saws ran only from 6:00 A.M. until noon on the sixth day. Old timers muttered, "*That*'s not a week's wuk!"

By 1900 Wesley worked in a store; by 1902 he farmed with his father-in-law, doing a week's wuk without a doubt; then for many years he farmed alone. I helped him out for a decade of summers, 1940 to 1950, and I must write about his

31

work-work-work, as I have written before; my recollection of Wesley Wells shines at the center of my life. I will write about him later, saving the best for last.

When I hear talk about "the work ethic" I puke. CEOs talk about it, whose annual salaries average one hundred and thirty times their workers' wages. Whatever the phrase purports to describe, it is not an ethic; it is not an idea of work's value or a moral dictate but a feeling or tone connected to work, and it is temperamental and cultural. Studs Terkel's stonemason has it, and his line-worker does not; instead, the line-worker has a work anger, or a work malevolence, which is entirely appropriate. Mind you, the stonemason works alone with his hands solving problems that change with every stone. He does something that he can look at and put his name to. He can measure what he has done in walls and buildings not in units of the same thing, like so many Chevrolet Impalas or so many distributor cap linings. Shades of John Ruskin. I no more have a work ethic than I have self-discipline. I have so many pages a day, so many books and essays.

Visiting my mother in Connecticut, I sit beside her recliner and she asks what I am up to. I tell her about *Life Work*. "I think your book will be *inspirational* to people," she responds; she has been building me up since I was born; but she has her own ego: "When I look around this house," she goes on, "I see so much that I have made. Drapes, curtains, bedspreads, most of the quilts. Not the blankets of course. Lace for the pillowcases." She points to the drapes in the sunroom where she lives waking and sleeping. "I made those drapes in 1938 and the edges are all worn. I hope they live longer than I do." After a moment she says, "I *know* the upstairs drapes need washing but I *can't*." In fact she cannot mount the stairs to see that they are dirty but she knows it well enough. Then she goes back to thinking of a life's work, shaped into objects throughout this house. "They are *mine*," she says.

All winter I find Jane standing by the dining-room windows looking into the secluded garden she has made behind the house; all winter she plans next summer's back garden. On mild days in March she begins cleaning the garden patch for the better days coming; when we hear that the temperature will drop below freezing again—March, April, even May— she covers or recovers bulbs and emerging snowdrops with mulch from last year's leaves. Snowdrops, daffodils, tulips, roses, peonies, hollyhocks, lilies. All summer she works every day that it does not rain, and sometimes she works in rain. She works on poems early at her desk, when the garden is wet with dew, or she might not write at all in summer. By nine-thirty or ten she is outside armed with spoons and spades, trimming and feeding, helping and preparing. On late warm evenings of June and July, only darkness forces her inside. She gardens twelve hours a day, some days.

And her flowers reward her work by their magnificence: peonies whiter than the idea of white and as big as basketballs; hollyhocks seven feet tall with a blossom delicately peach-pink. People swerve and slow down driving by, if they are flower people; we fear accidents.

I call it work and so does Jane although it is voluntary and produces no revenue—except when, in bare cold November or a rainy stretch of June, Jane writes a poem or an essay out of her gardening. Her garden is work because it is a devotion undertaken with passion and conviction; because it absorbs her; because it is a task or unrelenting quest which cannot be satisfied. True gardening is atavistic and represents or embodies or fulfills the centuries or millennia that her ancestors (all of our ancestors) spent working in dirt. Our forefathers and foremothers farmed not for pleasure but to stay alive or to satisfy the Squire, to survive on leavings from milord's table or to lay up sheepswool and turnips to sustain themselves through the snows of winter. Whatever the source or motive for their work, the hymns of dirt-work continue their chorus below the level of our consciousness.

As we look back across millennia, we see a social structure that is largely agricultural. Although many males from fourteen to fifty fight in the emperor's army or climb the rigging of the emperor's ships, the remaining males together with children and women plough, dig, plant seed, carry water, weed, and harvest. Thus in the suburbs we rake leaves together; thus we trim the forsythia; thus we arrange a sprinkler on the suburban lawn, edge the grass neatly against the sidewalk, mow, and mulch. If we could look from outer space down on North America on an August Saturday, we would watch a suburban nation of farmers tending tiny plots. Canceling time, or standing at a telescope further out in space, we would watch multitudes in 1000 B.C. growing wheat in Mesopotamia. In the city apartment when we raise African violets in the window we plant wheat beside the Nile. In Connecticut the millionaire in his modern house with a swimming pool spends one day a week driving his tractor—he could hire it done a thousand times over—to mow the smooth acres of his estate. He is never so happy—not playing bridge that night drinking Chivas, not reading the *Journal* over coffee or estimating his net worth at the market's close—as he is while he bumps over lawn on his Farmall, master of his lands gathering his weekly harvest.

Who is worst-off, for work, in human history? When I read Studs Terkel's *Working* I choose our nomadic Mexican farm laborers, laboring in the fields from early childhood until death, days sometimes elongated to seventeen hours. When I read Richard Henry Dana's *Two Years Before the Mast* I switch to sailors in nineteenth century merchant fleets: They never spent more than four hours in bed and usually worked a sixteen-hour day (longer in danger; and don't forget the danger) often seven days a week, away from land for months and from home for years at a time. Then I think of the soldier, legionary or hoplite marching all night to fight at dawn, hardtack and salt beef and what you can loot. I have not mentioned slavery, and the history of humanity is the history of slavery. Mind you, in some cultures or historical eras slaves were better off than gentleman soldiers. But the chattel slavery of the Americans, perpetuated until late in the Christian era, I propose as the nineteenth century's equivalent to Hitler's and Stalin's exterminations. Or read *Das Kapital*—or any objective history of the same period—and compare the labors of miners or factory workers in England—often women and children—with labors of the felaheen in the Old Kingdom.

Work is what we do to feed ourselves and keep ourselves warm. Some hunter-gatherers, in a fortunate climate with fortunate vegetation, can work twelve hours a week—leaving the rest of their time for lovemaking, magic, religion, gossip, games, and drinking the local brew. Watching television ads during sports events, I note that we aspire to the condition of this hunter-gatherer. D. H. Lawrence wrote that "for some mysterious or obvious reason, the modern woman and the modern man hate physical work," and "The dream of every man is that in the end he shall have to work no more." When there is work in the TV advertisement, it is something done quickly—and the reward is drinking beer. Do we want a house? A house goes up in twenty seconds in a crafted sequence of thirty shots; we watch the house rise as we watch a flower open when the camera takes a frame every four hours over two days. These work-ads remind me of my dreams of gardening, which never included a sore back, in which I never dropped a hoe or misplaced a trowel; in television ads no one is tired, and no one is old. The hunting-gathering TV young, all slim and beautiful and energetic, gather to drink and dance and flirt at the Silver Bullet, aka the Earthly Paradise. We understand that centuries of off-stage labor, not to mention evolution and history and civilization and the opposable thumb, have brought us to this time and moment of sexual leisure. We also understand the hunting-gathering young must have a life-expectancy like a slave's in a Hittite galley, because nobody here is as old as twenty-seven.

Lawrence writing seventy years ago foresaw the Silver Bullet. "It means, apart from the few necessary hours of highly paid and congenial labor, that men and women shall have nothing to do except enjoy themselves. No beastly housework for the women, no beastly homework for the men. Free! free to enjoy themselves. More films, more motor-cars, more dances, more golf, more tennis and more getting completely away from yourself. And the goal of life is enjoyment."

Baudelaire on the other hand claimed that work was less

boring than amusing yourself. Surely I agree, but not everyone does: Enjoyment in the shape of golf absorbed my father as his work did not; work and its anxiety *engaged* him— but worry and dread do not characterize the absorbedness that Gurchuran Das described. Golf was an engaging pastime, and the atavistic sources of sport are as clear as the origins of lawncare: not agriculture but warfare.

Pastimes are always atavistic and they will not do for a life's structure. When work is utterly disagreeable, and week awaits weekend, our delight in recreation reveals our misery. The Silver Bullet, like the touch football game that precedes it, is the house of wretchedness. The goal of life is enjoyment? It depends on the quality of the joy; elsewhere Lawrence wrote, "It seems as if the great aim and purpose in human life were to bring all life into the human consciousness. And this is the final meaning of work: the extension of human consciousness." We understand: Not everyone can work to extend the consciousness of others. For most of us, the exercise of freedom—doing what we like doing—may best extend our own.

But the goal is worthy: As Swami Vivekananda says: "work like a *master* and not as a *slave*; work incessantly, but do not do slave's work. Do you not see how everybody works? Nobody can be altogether at rest; ninety-nine percent of mankind work like slaves, and the result is misery; it is all selfish work. Work through freedom! Work through love!"

When I hung around baseball's major leagues, talking to ballplayers, I discovered to my glee that ballplayers talked about work, just as poets do, in opposite ways. I brag about six hundred drafts of "Another Elegy"; John Ashbery, on the other hand—confronted with having written a poem in twenty minutes when he was an undergraduate—answers, "Yes. I took longer then." Half the athletes told me that working at baseball is silly; hell, just go out there and have fun . . . The other half said (and wholly believed) that they lacked any natural ability, that they accomplished their success by dint of practice, preparation, hard work, and virtue. In *The Boys of Summer* Roger Kahn remembered how George "Shotgun" Shuba—who hit line drives for the old Dodgers—told him of arduous practice all winter, convinced that only hard labor allowed him to play baseball. (If I had practiced twelve hours a day, at my physical peak, I would never have hit a line drive off a major league pitch.) Roger Kahn kept telling him, "But you're a natural," until Shuba finally reared up and contradicted him: "You talk like a sportswriter. In the winters, for fifteen years after loading potatoes or anything else, even when I was in the majors, I'd swing at the clump six hundred times." Shuba hung a ball of string from the ceiling of his basement and swung a bat at it: "after sixty I'd make an X. Ten Xs and I had my six hundred swings. Then I could go to bed. . . . I swung a 44-ounce bat 600 times a night, 4,200 times a week, 47,200 swings every winter."

In spring training of 1992, Roger Clemens showed up in excellent physical shape, and then stepped up his preparations. On Florida days when he went five innings, he ran a mile and a half *before* pitching. He explained that he was toughening himself for late in the season, or even late in a game when he had to pitch tired. Between innings, in Winter Haven, he left the mound not to rest in the dugout but to do sit-ups; or he recruited a coach to throw him pick-ups— low ground balls which he fielded first on one side and then on the other. Asked why he worked so hard he answered, "People write articles about how you're *blessed* with the right arm . . . That might be true, for some people, but I had to work to get where I'm at."

Five years ago I put in my satellite dish, and every night after work I watch a game, or more likely part of a game; by the sixth or seventh inning, sleepiness overtakes me. August through January, some nights (or afternoons) I watch football, but baseball is my favorite, with basketball a lively second. Before I installed the dish, I listened to radio baseball on weeknights and watched ghostly games on weekends. Saturday afternoons for decades I have paid my bills watching television sports; I have looked through magazines, put photographs into albums, worked on my income tax—done all sorts of desultory tasks (not work) that reward full attention with full boredom. With the advent of the dish, I watch every Red Sox game, every Celtics game, and when my teams aren't playing I watch other teams—finding more wearisome chores to accomplish, to cross off my list:

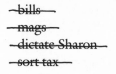

When I put in the dish, it was bliss; it remains bliss. Everyone needs to let the inner child out, to undertake some mildly pleasant activity that absorbs or engages us only a little. Writing leaves me high; I need to come down. Years ago, whiskey did it; but there are side effects: bruises, adultery, liver failure, divorce. Yeats read Zane Grey at night, Eliot Agatha Christie. I do not claim a superior sensibility but junk prose gives me hives. Nor can I sit still for movies or talk shows; but for sports, intellectually equivalent to *The Price is Right* or Judith Krantz, I sit with my mouth open, witlessly enraptured—as long as I have one other thing to do while watching. When the bliss dish started to deliver, with amusement Jane watched me watching. At first she decided that, having achieved nirvana, I would never strive again. "They'll say, 'Whatever became of Hall?'" Then she thought again, and decided that I would use the dish in order to do more work.

First of all I sleep less. I still get up from 4:30 to 5:15 in the morning; I work the same day's routine, but I used to go to bed at 8:30 or 9:00—reading, getting sleepy, going to sleep. In the old days, I often woke to read from one to two, which I seldom do any more; now, I read another hour in the afternoon, and because I spend less time in bed read and write more hours a day. There are books I dip into between pitches—not Gibbon, not George Herbert—when I need to look through something but fullest attention would go unrewarded. Mostly, I dictate letters. I used to dictate in the late morning or afternoon but now I dictate almost entirely during sporting events (I tell my friends, "It's tied in the tenth!") and save the daylight hours for . . . for *work*, as I call it. In the low bookcase beside my blue chair, where I sit watching sports, I have secreted a Sony dictator. Every night at 7:30 I fit myself to the TV's sound by way of an earplug, pick up the day's mail, and address myself to friends. To Paul Minnie Avenue in Santa Cruz, I say "Dear Adrienne . . ." I average five thousand letters and postcards every year. Once when the mailman was late I bit his leg.

There are days, there are days.

The best day begins with waking early—I check the clock: damn!, it's only 3:00 A.M.—because I want so much to get out of bed and start working. Usually something particular beckons so joyously—like a poem that I have good hope for, that seems to go well. Will it look as happy today as it looked yesterday? I roll over to wait, to take a nap at 3:00 A.M., because getting up at three will wreck the day. I close my eyes and doze, waking to check the clock every twenty-seven minutes. By four-thirty I can wait no longer. I leap out of bed, feed the cat, let the dog out, start the coffee which is timed for five but can be persuaded of an early start, dress, drive two miles for the *Globe*, carry a cup of coffee to Jane, read the paper while I eat a blueberry bagel, then finish my breakfast with skim milk, an apple, and a small peanut butter sandwich. I wake as I eat, drink, and read the paper. As I approach the end of the *Globe*, saving the sports section until last, I feel work-excitement building, joy-pressure mounting—until I need resist it no more but sit at the desk and open the folder that holds the day's beginning, its desire and its hope.

Then I lose myself. In the best part of the best day, *absorbedness* occupies me from footsole to skulltop. Hours or minutes or days—who cares?—lapse without signifying. When I have done as much as I can on the moment's poem, I move to another. Depending on their lengths, I work on one poem or I work on five or even ten. At any moment when a poem does not occupy me wholly, when I feel impatient or discouraged or tired, I drop it quickly; after a while—one hour, three hours?—I feel the poetry-juices drying out. Instantly I stop; I put the poems away until the following morning.

Now I need to interrupt work with a chore. In the years before we installed an oil furnace, I carried logs from the woodshed to various stoves. Now I make another cup of coffee; or I take the mail out to the box. When I have dawdled a sufficient blank space after poetry-time, I am ready to move to prose. There's a new children's book that I've taken from my mother's recollection of childhood Christmases; I do another draft, changing little things, wondering if the end is conclusive. There's my book review of Tom Williams, third draft and fairly inchoate, which I trim here and expand there and revise sentence-by-sentence; this piece will take many drafts; I don't know why. My essay on graveyards goes better; its second draft is further along than the fifth draft of the book review. There's my proposal that local art agencies judge and sponsor publication of local writers in local newspapers. I make a new draft for each of these small endeavors. There is also *Life Work*; today I save it for later.

This morning, when I have worked over as much prose as I wish to, when I feel tired, it is 10:00 A.M. I've been up five and a half hours, and over the last four hours I have done my day's work. It's 10:00 A.M. and the rest of the day is gravy. If it's gravy, it's also a touch boring; through mid-day, through afternoon and evening until I go to sleep, I will look forward to tomorrow morning and the 6:00 A.M. desk. But I cannot fake it in the afternoon; if I push too hard, I become impatient and do bad work.

Ernest Hemingway makes a model of the good day:

When I am working on a book or a story I write every morning as soon after first light as possible. There is no one to disturb you and it is cool or cold and you come to your work and warm as you write. You read what you have written and, as you always stop when you know what is going to happen next, you go on from there. You write until you come to a place where you still have your juice and know what will happen next and you stop and try to live through until the next day when you hit it again. You have started at six in the morning, say, and may go on until noon or be through before that. When you stop you are as empty, and at the same time never empty but filling, as when you have made love to someone you love. Nothing can hurt you, nothing can happen, nothing means anything until the next day when you do it again. It is the wait until the next day that is hard to get through.

At ten I dictate up the changes I've made on manuscript poems and prose, add a tape of letters I did during baseball the night before, and deliver to Lois the afternoon's typing and word processing. Now I shave, if I didn't shave earlier. I read a manuscript by a friend who wants advice—or praise; who wants mostly praise, but who will receive some blame, some praise, and some advice—and proofread the index of *Their Ancient Glittering Eyes*, the new prose book that comes out next August.

Eleven o'clock, and time for lunch. When you eat breakfast at five-thirty, you eat lunch at eleven: cheese, bread, V-8, and raisins. I eat raisins while I read in bed beside Jane, getting drowsy towards our twenty-minute naps. All morning Jane has done things parallel and different: breakfast, reading the Upanishads, dog-walk, desk work on poems, maybe some letters. We do not speak all morning, but her presence in her own study, working as I work, means everything to my work. When she is away doing a poetry reading I am lethargic, moony, and blue; I work a slow-down half-speed schedule: work-to-order, blue flu. I invent reasons to leave the house on errands; I fill out coupons for magazines and join book clubs.

On this best day Jane is home and I have no errands. We wake from our naps at the same time, and by earlier agreement know what we will do next. How nice to be old enough, living together and alone, to make love in daylight with no more precaution than taking the phone off the hook.

Buzzing with love's drug I walk the dog, twenty minutes a day. Jane acquired Gus largely to force me to leave the house while moving my legs. Otherwise there were always good reasons why, today, I should read a book or go back to the desk instead of taking a walk. Walking Gus on the best day, the countryside is beautiful. If we climb the dirt New Canada Road early in October, I gaze open-mouthed into the deep mixed woods that do what they always do: birches slim and delicate with yellow leaves, stout black-green hemlock, ash and popple and the rare elm, over all the sugar maple's violent red. As he runs Gus kicks up red and yellow leaves that mark the dirt underneath with their bright signatures.

We walk the same road most days all year, and the walk is different always. In dead winter the sky is densely blue, tree shadows sharp on the white earth, stone walls revealed in the absence of leaves, granite boulders and evergreens. In spring when New Canada is muddy we walk the paved but untraveled Walker Brook Road where the trout stream roars in continuous outrage. Or in high summer we walk the abandoned track of the railroad picking wild raspberries from bushes that tug at my trousers and shirt. Gus doesn't care, summer or winter; rain or snow. He is cheerful, walking and sniffing, leaping with great bounds like a deer and stopping short when he encounters a seductive odor. It is not work, walking the dog; because I put it on my list it must be a chore, a beautiful chore. My only annoyance, walking, comes when my mind willy-nilly forms sentences. Larking as I look, I hear myself think: "leaves that mark the dirt underneath with their bright signatures." I tell myself to *shut up*; *stop the writing* for a while.

Back from the walk I bring in the mail and sit in my blue chair to read it: long letters from three old friends; five letters from acquaintances; eight brief notes about free-lancer business—a vita required for a poetry reading, an invitation to submit to a magazine, a request for a book review, a feeler about a bookstore appearance, a note from a publisher asking for a blurb; manuscripts from two strangers; proof of a poem for a magazine; two new poetry books; four magazines; and a box containing twenty copies of a remaindered book: my book: grump. I read the letters and tuck them beside my chair where I keep the dictator.

Then what do I do? This time of the day is lowest energy for me, not sleepy but slow-witted and lacking in drive or purpose. I look forward to tomorrow morning; I distribute a pile of books and magazines, tidying a little; I lie back in bed and pick up the book I went to sleep by, Studs Terkel as it happens, and read for half an hour. Rarely do I feel sleepy enough to take another nap. Maybe I invent an errand even if I don't have one: I will arise and go now to the supermarket, or put gas in the car, or deposit a check at the bank. I read some more, not only *Working* but Robert Creeley's *Selected Poems* or Harry Matthews' *Cigarettes* or Meister Eckhart. Jane and I drink a cup of decaf. I read more manuscript for a friend; I read manuscript for a publisher, who will pay me a hundred and fifty dollars for reading three hundred pages and writing him a letter. Then, at four o'clock, energy comes back, energy and enterprise together. I sit at my desk again and draft eight hundred words of *Life Work*—about the best day—and put it on tomorrow's tape for Lois.

Between five and six the Concord *Monitor* arrives and I sit in my blue chair reading a newspaper again. I look at magazines until dinner, which is Indian vegetarian ever since Jane and I returned from India last November. Jane cooks with imagination and resourcefulness, reconciling flavor with my diabetes. We go back and forth saying grace. Today is my turn and I say the couplet I made up: "Dear Lord, accept our gratitude / For this long day, and for our food." I clear the supper table, rinse the dishes, and put them in the dishwasher, my heavy-duty housework for the day. I put the dog out. I dash down to Lois's house and bring back the afternoon's typing. (Clean copy of this morning's work sits on my desk for tomorrow.) I bring tomorrow morning's clean clothes to set them on top of the parlor Glenwood. When we lived without central heat I learned to dress and undress by the woodstove, and I still dress and undress there—although the Glenwood has been cold for eight years except when the oil company messes up. I fix the morning coffee, storing water in one place and frozen beans in another, pressing buttons to command the hour of grinding. I take out my upper partial and assemble tooth-cleaning apparatus beside my chair.

At seven-thirty, as the Red Sox arrive at the tube from outer space—Spacenet Three, Transponder Three—I read through the letters I dictated the night before, correcting and signing them, explaining or expanding in an illegible script. Dictator's errors are notorious, when you say one thing and it comes back something else. It is expedient to read your letters over before you mail them. Our mailing address is Eagle Pond Farm and two letters have arrived mislabeled, sort of, by correspondents who dictate. Former announcer of Red Sox baseball on radio, Ken Coleman, wrote me at Evil Pond Farm, an address I admire for its Stephen King touch. My favorite, however, is the inadvertent truth on the envelope of a letter from Stephen Jay Gould who addressed me (arguing a baseball point) at Ego Pond Farm.

Jane and I watch a few innings. She *watches*, if she watches. If she has something else to do—like writing a letter or looking at a magazine or listening to music—she shuts out the game. One world at a time for Jane as for Henry David Thoreau. Sometimes I tuck the sound in my ear and she reads on the sofa. Always while watching I do a second thing—flossing my teeth, looking through the weekly *Argus Champion* or *PW*, checking out the QPBC catalog for anything about work. Then Jane disappears into the bathroom to take out her lenses and attend to her skin. I plug the Red Sox into my ear, if I'm not already plugged, turn on my Sony, pick up the microphone and chat with my friends.

Or I tend to business, postcards and brief letters: I'm sorry but I don't do blurbs; I'm sorry that I cannot talk to the children at your school but I've taken on four schools this spring; the proof looks just fine but in line twelve please change "and" to "but"; I can come to the bookstore Friday the twelfth, four to six, on my way back from the airport—if the plane's on time; I'm sorry but I can't read your manuscript now; I'm sorry that it will take me four months before I can read your manuscript. Or I write a researcher to ask about books on work; or I write an editor asking her *please* to tell me what's going on with a manuscript I sent eight weeks ago; I write another editor with an idea about the design of a book. Then, maybe, I answer the letters of friends and acquaintances, responding to their news and adding my own. I tell them, "the game's still tied in the eleventh."

On the best day, I have enough strength to watch the game through, flossing in the eighth inning, and during a change of pitchers putting gel on my few remaining teeth. I look through *The Nation*; I look through half of *The New Criterion*. I pick up my Day-Timer and list things for tomorrow:

> poems
> prose
> call Philippa about Friday
> call about eye appointment
> Celtics tickets with Andrew
> New London, shop and pick up camera
> *Life Work*

We win it in the last of the twelfth, on the best day—when we lose I am disconsolate for ninety seconds; baseball woe fades fast—as I undress and put on my nightshirt. When I go to bed I read twenty pages of *Working* before my eyes refuse to remain open.

The best day depends partly on other people. Jane's presence, working in her study on her poems, enables me to concentrate on my own. But also, "I dash down to Lois's house and bring back the afternoon's typing." Until 1960 or so, I typed my own manuscripts. Often I worked directly onto the typewriter but I came to think that it was bad for my work. I typed rapidly—one finger and many errors—and tended to run on, to be glib and glibber, never to pause and x-out or reconsider. For me, the typewriter was mania; when I wrote longhand I slowed down; I paused to cross something out and to try again. But then, in order to read and revise, I needed to type from my handwriting; then I would mess the page up with my handwriting again, then type it again . . . The mechanics took time—my impatience was with mechanics not with revision—and when I typed my back hurt.

Someone told me about a good typist in town, and tentatively I began to take her my work. Dorothy Foster became my friend as well as my keyboard-helper and typed for me off and on for thirty years (I mailed manuscripts from New Hampshire). Dorothy loved to type, loved her own speed, accuracy, and shrewdness in solving problems of wretched penmanship; she took the same list-making, crossing-out pleasure in work as I did. And when I hired Dorothy to type manuscript, I found that I did more work; I had withheld myself from the desk because typing was painful and boring. As businessmen say, "You have to spend money to make money." By selling one more essay or book review a year, I paid for Dorothy's hours.

Then I discovered dictation. The Department of English at the University of Michigan possessed a spare Grundig Stenorette, available to teachers for dictating letters of reference. I tried, and at first my sentences sounded like a witless parody of Winston Churchill, pompous and wandering. (Ford Madox Ford said that Theodore Watts-Dunton "addressed me as if I were a public meeting.") I used the dictated originals as drafts and tried again; in a mere two weeks of reference-writing season, I learned to dictate letters that sounded as natural as anything I pecked on my typewriter or scrawled in my illegible longhand—although I needed to supply "comma" and even "exclamation point!" as well as to spell proper names. I have dictated ever since. Living in the country, preferring solitude, we entertain few visitors and never go to dinner parties; but gregariousness withered in the flesh blooms in the post: thus my five thousand annual pieces of mail.

Many helpers have typed from my dictation. In Ann Arbor for years it was Sharon Giannotta; the year Jane and I moved to New Hampshire, Sharon moved to California with her neurosurgeon husband. Twenty years later, she types an hour's tape every week. In New Hampshire Lois Fierro, who lives seven-tenths of a mile south in West Andover, types five days a week—a maximum of four hours, an average of two and a half hours a day. Lately, Lois types my letters on an IBM Selectric II and reproduces manuscript on an IBM clone with Word-Perfect; every morning I mess up fresh copy. Lois doesn't drive, her kids are grown, and her husband Gene leaves for work mid-afternoon. Alone, she helps me out, an arrangement that benefits us both. With her income from typing she and Gene travel; once we met for a pub lunch in Devonshire.

In Ann Arbor I walked by the university library, traveling from my house to the classroom. If I needed to check a fact, I would stop by. Here, I have a large reference library but it's not always adequate. Did Prescott Bush inherit his money or make it? How long did it take a sailing ship to travel from Boston to Calcutta in the nineteenth century? When I need library help, I hire men and women to look things up, to xerox pages or postcard a date. It saves me time that I would otherwise spend on the road driving to libraries in Concord or Hanover. Sometimes two researchers work for me at once; always two or three people type. On my staff, as it were, no one works more than a few hours a week, but the staff's labor saves me hours by the dozen—freeing me to work, helping me to manufacture the best day.

Henry Moore is a model for work. I met him first in 1959 when I lived with my family for a year in an English village about fifteen miles from Moore's house. I had first known Moore for his shelter drawings; and as an undergraduate I thumbtacked to my Eliot House wall a Penguin Print of a study for sculpture. In 1951, coming to Europe for the first time, I saw many of his sculptures outdoors (where they stand in happy competition with the natural world) at the Festival of Britain. In 1959 the American magazine *Horizon* commissioned me to conduct an interview with him, *Paris Review* style. That year, on leave without pay from the university, I lived by my wits for the first time—BBC work, reviews for the *New Statesman* and *Encounter*, an encyclopedia of poetics co-edited with Stephen Spender—and the interview would contribute to the family budget. I wrote him a letter with the suggestion; he asked me for tea to talk about it, and I took a bus from Thaxted to Bishop's Stortford seven miles from his house and studios that occupied Hertfordshire farmland. He met the bus in his Rover, generous to take time away from work, and after tea agreed to be interviewed. We met two or three times again, sitting in his living room with a tape recorder between us. He and I played Ping-Pong. He and his wife Irina drove to our house for dinner.

Irina was a beautiful and intelligent woman whom Henry had met when she was an art student and Henry a teacher, who had given up her drawing to concentrate on gardening, who loved silence and solitude. Moore was gregarious by nature, but in their household she led the way: Solitude won out over company, which satisfied another powerful portion of Henry Moore, because he loved dearly to work. If he had married a woman who enjoyed society and conversation, Moore would have wasted his time at parties. He wanted most to get up in the morning, pick up a piece of clay, and work all day into the night. His work was various: modeling new ideas in a little old studio filled with oddly shaped pebbles, old maquettes, and bone; working over waxes that came from the foundry before they returned to become bronzes; carving in stone or wood; sketching; or overseeing assistants, young sculptors who translated models into larger versions—six inches to three feet, three feet to fourteen, fourteen to twenty-seven. Maybe I felt free to hire typists and researchers because Henry hired assistants.

Moore interrupted himself for lunch, tea, drinks, and supper; for mail, although mail was a burden; for the telephone; for the founder's truck that came to haul away a great plaster for casting. All day he rode a bicycle over his acreage in the rolling farmland, patrolling his studios to work on different projects. At night after supper he and Irina might watch a BBC detective mystery, but as he watched he kept a pad open on his lap and made automatic or random marks in pencil— and sometimes ideas derived from his idle doodles. When I last saw him at eighty he had built a new graphic studio next to the house, where he retreated for an hour after television, working again between nine and ten at night.

Moore did not arrive among the rich and the famous until he was in his forties. Earlier, he had taught for a living, sculpting as much as he could the rest of the day in a Hampstead studio, or at a cottage in the country during holidays. He grew up in Castleford near Leeds, where his father was a coal miner who swore that none of his children would ever go down to the pits. They didn't—except when Henry sketched coal mining during the Second World War; most of the children taught school, as Henry might have done if he had not served in the Great War and attended art school, first in Leeds and then at the Royal Academy, on something like the G.I. Bill. His whole life felt lucky to him, to have escaped the pits for the studio, to have traded work at the surface of a coal seam for work at the surface of marble and alabaster, of wood and clay.

Although he refused to attend some openings, others took him away from his work; so did lectures, which he mostly refused, and ceremonial occasions and honorary degrees or investitures. Celebrity dogged him and he fought it. Yet he gave up work one afternoon for a photo session, or a morning for a meeting of the directors of the Tate Gallery. During the years when I knew him he was celebrated all over the world, and he enjoyed his fame no end, but remained vigilant to combat its cost in work. I returned three years after the interview to do his *New Yorker* profile, and again when he was eighty for another magazine piece. He wrote me postcards and letters from time to time (I bought etchings; I lectured about him and required slides, which he provided; or he just said hello.) Always he asked me to drop by when I visited England, but we dropped by only twice, because I understood that although his invitations were genuine we would interrupt his day. Only once did I feel impatience from him—he wanted to be working—when Jane and I came calling in the autumn after his summer had been wasted by the huge show in Florence in the 1970s.

The last time I saw him I cherish. He talked about his new grandson and showed us drawings in a studio he had just built to extend his workday. We sat with a drink in the sunny living room he had added to the house which, when he moved to it during the war, had been a broken-down farmworker's cottage. I knew my man, and I asked him, "Now that you're eighty, you must know the secret of life. What is the secret of life?" With anyone else the answer would have begun with an ironic laugh, but Henry Moore answered me straight: "The secret of life is to have a task, something you devote your entire life to, something you bring everything to, every minute of the day for your whole life. And the most important thing is—it must be something you cannot possibly do!"

Henry Moore's work was the high road of art, and the "something you cannot possibly do" was to be the greatest sculptor who ever lived and know it. What did it have to do with directing the bronze-founder's flatbed trailer through a narrow lane past Irina's garden to a twenty-five-foot plaster cast? Or with sitting in front of *Z-Cars* moving a soft pencil over a pad? Not all a person's work is the high road, even if that person is Henry Moore. Even Henry Moore must hurry to finish work on a plaster, to roll it under cover as the thunder starts; must pay his taxes; must get to the train on time. What exactly *is* the sculptor's work? Surely it is not his or her work to submit to the photo session or to come up with words of thanks for the queen when she bestows the Order of Merit. These are trivial by-products of the task to be a sculptor better than Donatello. How do you *express* the task? What is common to it, what is the general nature of the consciousness that undertakes it? Henry interviewed spoke of "form-knowledge" and "form-experience." Certainly his eye, or more accurately his hand, made concrete and beautiful the shapes and volumes of the world's material, following forms of the creation.

My own high road is to make poems better than Dante, Homer, and Virgil, not to mention folks closer to home like

Whitman, Dickinson, Frost, Stevens, and Kinnell. My own day's work, on the best day, does not directly confront this task for more than two hours, or rarely three. When I head for the airport parking lot, on my way to read my poems at Pocatello, I pay the task's mortgage as I display the materials of the task. But flying to Idaho I am not *accomplishing* anything. More clearly—because more like and most ridiculously unlike—I do not confront Milton or Tu Fu when I compose a headnote for an essay collection used in composition classes:

> John McPhee (b. 19xx) grew up in Princeton, New Jersey, where he now resides. After working for *Time*, McPhee joined the staff of the *New Yorker* for which he crafts his meticulous . . .

Nor do I contend with Edward Gibbon when I revise these words, in horror and humiliation over my stereotypical formulae and graceless rhythm:

> John McPhee (b. 1931) lives in Princeton, New Jersey, where he was born and attended the University. He began as an anonymous journalist of fact, writing for *Time*, and has become the maestro of a factual music composed for the *New Yorker* . . .

In truth . . . I love the revising and the messing about. Granted that this work is not the work I care most about, it resembles my work; then what is my work?

Six years ago I spent seven weeks away from the desk as Jane and I talked our way through China and Japan for USIS. I knew I would miss work; it had been eleven years since I had taken more than a day or two away, when Jane and I moved house from Michigan to New Hampshire. I figured it might be good for my work—this enforced interruption in an exciting pursuit—and that I would return full of beans. (It happened: manic energy once jet lag flew away.) For seven weeks of travel I wrote nothing except one hundred and four postcards, a literary form I have never mastered. Toward the end I felt desk-energy accumulate, not as desire to write about China and Japan, not as desire to address a particular topic or return to a particular poem, but simply as desire to work with words again. Our last public day before flying home we visited the Hokkaido Historical Museum in Sapporo, and the generous director himself took us around—busy like all Japanese; compact or dense with things to accomplish; pointing out among other historical relics farm implements that were identical to the pitchforks and scythes that my grandfather and I used forty years before, during the war with Japan. The director took us to lunch and after noodle soup asked an embarrassed favor. His English was excellent; he pulled from his pocket a sheet of paper on which he had typed two lines of English, a caption he needed to supply for a photograph. Would we check grammar and idiom?

Sure enough he had omitted an article expected in English; I supplied it, with a caret. Then I saw that the second of his two short sentences would sound better turned around, with the verb at the end; then I saw that I could combine the two sentences into one complex sentence, saving a third of the words and making the style more condensed and elegant . . . I was in heaven! On a plastic tabletop in Sapporo I moved language to and fro, playing with words, changing their order or position and altering nuances of vocabulary, syntax, rhythm, . . . for what purpose? Oh, *to make it better*—though I would be hard put to explain or prove my comparative.

The arts do not duplicate each other by analogy; nor do I claim to resemble Henry Moore in ability or even in ambition—but let me assert that Moore's equivalent to my Hokkaido caption is the perception and manipulation of forms, shapes, and volumes. When Moore saw granite poking through the ground in woods, his eyes took the stone in, texture and weight. I watched him as he spoke sometimes, holding a pebble's weight in his stubby fingers, rolling it back and forth, loving it and *taking it in* through the nerves under his skin. I watched him absently rearrange objects on a table—ashtrays, boxes, pencils—and alter their relationships in space. When he looked at a sheep or a cloud; or at salt and pepper shakers on a supper table; or at an elephant's skull; or at the founder's flatbed trailer; or at the photographer's Nikon, he saw edges and shapes and weights. Form-perception filled the constant breathing moments of his dedicated life.

Barry Moser and I will do children's books together. We have met once only, and begin to know each other by letter. Collaboration can be difficult, or disastrous, even when one artist works in sentences and the other in pigment. We need each to develop a feeling for the other, what the other loves and hates, what he is best at. Just now, he has sent me the draft of a lecture he will deliver to the American Booksellers' Association, and I feel the pleasure and relief of affinity. "I'm up between six and seven," Moser says, "make coffee, feed the dogs, cats, and occasionally my granddaughter. I sit down at my drawing table by eight, and begin my work designing, drawing, painting, engraving, or doing calligraphy. I work until 11:30 or thereabouts, at which time I go to fetch my mail, grab a sandwich, do my shopping for the evening meal, run my errands, and get back to my drawing table by about one o'clock. Then I work till the sun goes over the yard arm, which on my hill comes somewhere between five and seven in the evening. This is a seven day schedule for fifty or so weeks out of the year. . . ."

Writers envy visual artists their muscular activity. Writers sit at desks and die early. Painters and sculptors work all day moving about, tapping, chiseling, modelling, mixing paints, and live to be ninety-seven praising work. Visual artists say the best things about work: Georgia O'Keeffe said, "The days you work are the best days." "Work is paradise," said Matisse. "To work," said Rodin, "is to live without dying." "You have to be with the work," said Louise Nevelson, "and the work has to be with you. It absorbs you totally and you absorb it totally."

There is work and work, for the visual artist as for others. Years ago when I spent some hours with artists in England—Eduardo Paolozzi, Jim Dine, Philip King, Isaac Witkin, R. J. Kitaj, even Francis Bacon—I was surprised by their general knowledge. Then I discovered that many of them kept BBC radio Home Service on all day as they worked. I cannot listen to *All Things Considered* while writing, but the examples are nonparallel because for me word would compete with word. I suspect that for an intellectual painter like Kitaj, radio-distraction may help by occupying the surface of the mind and allowing the hand a greater spontaneity of invention. Gertrude Stein sometimes wrote parked in her Ford at a busy intersection in Paris where French law required all drivers to squeeze their klaxons as they approached cross-streets—

because, as she said, the clangor took the top of her mind away.

On the other hand, painters or poets or CEOs—everybody in the world—can fool themselves by a busy laziness, like the "false hustle" Red Auerbach observed in athletes who pretend to give out more than they give. Henry Moore felt the middle-aged worker's contempt for young artists who could not manage more than an hour or two of labor a day. But he was wary as well of work's deceit. A sculptor can tap-tap-tap all day and night, he often said, and remain lazy. It's this deception that I fear for myself. I pile pages and add lines, I accumulate publication; maybe I use numbers to prove to an internalized authority that Donald is a good boy and has finished his homework, stacked the wood, fetched the eggs, washed the car, and weeded the cabbages. Now please can he go to bed (or whack his doodle) without reproach?

Adam and Eve were hunter-gatherers. Agriculture is the fall of man, raising and caring for flocks of animals or tilling the soil to raise crops—and it is a fall because it introduces work; God said so: "in the sweat of thy face shalt thou eat bread. . . ." Bread is a major metaphor of the Bible, Old Testament and New. We ask for bread and are given a stone. Jesus's flesh is bread, and transubstantiation makes metaphor literal. First bread is sustenance; then as metonomy it is one class of nutriment for all; then nutriment moves from bodies to souls.

Metaphor over the aeons has given folks trouble. Thus in the Living Bible Isaiah—who spoke of "bread" in older translations—asks, "why spend your money on foodstuffs?"

Maybe *labor* is the fall, not *work*. Hannah Arendt's distinction in *The Human Condition* is both fundamental and fundamentally obscured by the culture of our century: "the distinction between productive and unproductive labor contains . . . the more fundamental distinction between work and labor. It is indeed the mark of all laboring that it leaves nothing behind. . . ." Culture's thrust has twisted our language: "From the standpoint of 'making a living,' every activity unconnected with labor becomes a 'hobby.'"

The best day has its corollary. When I draw back from making these sentences, to think about the book I am making—as I walk the dog or drive the car—I worry that my enthusiasm over work, over the best day (over my own life, over the way I choose to live) will seem to a saturnine or grumpy reader the ultimate in complacency—complacency raised to the point of monstrosity. Why is happiness unforgivable? It is, and my sanguine temperament as I write about work alters the day's progress into a vision as idealized as de Crevecoeur's when he imagines his American farmer; or as Addison and Steele's when they invent the benign Sir Roger de Coverley; or as Henry Adams's creating maryolatrous Normans; or as John Ruskin's and Ezra Pound's fabricating Renaissance Princes. I make for myself a golden age.

Only depressives make a golden age; or maniacs create a golden age because their dark brother lurks behind the barn.

The best day is real—but takes its power and its energy from the urgency of its contradiction. It is not only blood chemistry that dictates ups and downs but the circumstances of anybody's life. What is the worst day? One worst day is the blank page of apathy or depression, when like Oblomov we see no reason to get out of bed. I remember lying alone in a bed smoking cigarettes, reading the cracks in the ceiling; for two years of middle life, my private life was a mess and I wrote no poems; depression rolled like the waves of mid-ocean day after day after day. Messages arrived coded into images and rhythms—I stuck some into notebooks—but I could not worry them onto the page, could not absorb myself at a desk. During these years I wrote a documentary play; I drafted a *New Yorker* profile of Henry Moore . . . but when I tried working on poems restlessness combined with nausea and anxiety: I could do nothing. Two years later, poetry made a brief return—but then three or four years afterwards (my late thirties and early forties) depression returned with a different face. I worked—desultorily, in short stretches—and finished things, and published them, but for six years I was aware that nothing I wrote was good enough; nothing was equal to a few things I had done earlier.

Again I came out of it, or so I believe, as the private life changed for the better. When Jane and I married and moved to New Hampshire I did my best work over a period of three or four years of gradually diminishing excitement. Sometimes in these years I panicked over money; would I be able to pay next year's tuition, or mortgage? Always something lucky turned up, like the *Ox-Cart Man* children's book, and panic faded while work-pleasure returned. Then my mood turned again: I wrote for five years—steadily, all day, free-lancing in New Hampshire—without the conviction or the sensation that my work was redeemable. I plugged along, working on certain longer poems for years, and the poems finally labored into what I wanted.

The worst day is the day when grief or sorrow overcome you. Your wife has cancer; you have cancer. Perhaps she will survive this engagement, perhaps you will, but the prospect of permanent estrangement darkens the day with curtains that let no light in. People happy in their work suffer like anyone else. Eight years ago Jane had cancer of the salivary gland—removed, and all clear by now; two and a half years ago I lost half my colon to a carcinoma. When I learned of my illness, I wept for myself and for my old mother, for my children and grandchildren, and for Jane. And I wept to think that I would have to stop working. This mortal curtailment of work-pleasure weighed less than the personal griefs—but it also weighed. When I went into the hospital I brought work with me, and in the last two days before I went home I started writing again. When I began to recover, still anxious about recurrence, I worked with a manic prolixity—not well—and knew in my heart that I worked against death. What's more, I realized that I had always worked—the real thing, the absorbedness—in defiance of death.

TWO

THESE LAST WORDS I wrote more than a week ago, and I wrote them on a Friday without consciousness of anxiety. Saturday I drove to Vermont and back, talking to teachers about children's books; it was a tense day because I drove through snow, rain, hail, ice, and more snow—on April 11. When I struggled home the mail had arrived with a happy message: The Guggenheim Foundation confirmed that Jane received a fellowship for her poems—great help at a time when the economy (even a free-lancer's) was failing; and more importantly a public acknowledgment of Jane's work. We celebrated quietly—but not for long. Sunday morning I worked on poems and on two small essays. Monday morning Jane and I left the house early for her appointment with Dr. Sutton, by coincidence the man who removed my colon cancer two and a half years ago. Jane has had a worsening pain in her tailbone, and one doctor suspected a cyst, which magnified in our imaginations. Dr. Sutton discovered no cyst or growth, but a genetic abnormality that left the tailbone liable to injury or soreness. We drove home with lessened anxiety to find a message on the machine; I should call my internist Dr. Clark. He had bad news: In my latest blood work-up, everything looked fine except the CEA, a blood protein which marks carcinoma. Before my colon surgery the CEA count had been a seven—anything over three is worrisome—and since my surgery it had been less than two. Today it was thirty-seven.

A scan Tuesday morning, read on Wednesday, showed something in the liver; it is the liver to which colon cancer metastasizes. Wednesday morning I watched the screen during ultrasound and saw the barbell shaped darkness on the liver's right lobe. No one *knows* what it is until pathology puts dyed cells under a microscope; but of course it is a metastatic lesion: Fatty tumors do not raise one's CEA. Today, Monday, a week after the CEA report, we see Dr. Sutton again. The issue now, given what we know, is the extent of the lesion or the presence of others not discernible by ultrasound. It is common that such cancer be pervasive throughout the liver; it is common that multiple metastatic lesions remain inoperable. One undertakes chemotherapy, but the cure rate for this disease is negligible. If I cannot be operated on, I will die fairly soon. A year? Eighteen months? Six months? I speculate; I cannot stop speculating.

But my internist and the ultrasound technician, looking at the barbell shape, claim that the rest of the liver looks clear—as do the kidneys and the spleen. They're not lying—but they know and I know that an ultrasound may not show everything. Later I discover that the barbell is one of the common shapes that a liver metastatis takes. The ultrasound technician describes it not as a barbell but as an hourglass. Ah, metaphor; do the sands run out? Maybe Dr. Sutton when he looks at the films this afternoon will find more lesions. If he operates, he may find more cancer when he opens me up and applies an operating room ultrasound to the surface of the liver itself. Possibly he can take out several little pieces; one can survive on a third of a liver, and there is something called the Swiss cheese operation. Or he can dis-

66

cover too many lesions to remove. I keep thinking of calves' liver on a butcher's tray, not sliced, cellophaned in a bag, slimy and warm-looking, twitching a little.

When I come out from anaesthetic, back in my room after the sojourn in ICU, I will open my eyes to ask Jane what they found. She will not lie to me.

If all goes well, as it were, I will by inches recover the morning *Globe*, the coffee, work on poems and work on prose, walking the dog, love with Jane, and the continual or recurrent dread—exacerbated every three months by checking my CEA—that a black cell multiplies. It is a common condition, for millions of people, old ones dropping off and new ones entering the mode: the cancer club, the deathwatch. Heaven knows (at moments of anxiety magic thinking knows no let or hindrance; *they* are reading everything I write on this yellow pad)—I'll take it, I'll take it.

The nature of this book alters. Shall I change the title from *Life Work* to *Work and Death*? Box office, he said sneering. Oh, let me return to my theme: I have worked all this pre-operation week but not on *Life Work*: I finished the graveyard (!) essay and the review of Tom Williams that I had almost finished; I finished another piece I had barely started; I wrote thirty letters canceling dates and postponing interviews or giving warnings; I drafted a letter to the National Council on the Arts because I must miss a critical meeting; with my editor's help I've revised phrases in *The Museum of Clear Ideas*, the poetry book scheduled for March of 1993; at Thom Gunn's suggestion I've added lines to the final section of "Another Elegy"; I've proofread *Their Ancient Glittering Eyes* again, and it looks clean. Like the left lobe of a liver? Absorbedness has helped and absorbedness is incomplete. This morning, as I write this medical report for *Life Work*, I find that work remains the matter, not only in defiance of death but in plain sight of it. It absorbs me to write these pages; it absorbs me more nearly than anything else has done for the past week or ten days. Writing about cancer allows me to transcend my cancer by the syntax or rhetoric of dread and suffering.

But then: I've been remembering—as I worked on "Another Elegy" and reviewed the posthumous collection of Tom Williams; as I finished my essay on graveyards—a quatrain that Stanley Kunitz wrote when he was in his twenties about his father who died before he was born:

> Observe the wisdom of the Florentine
> Who, feeling death upon him, scribbled fast
> To make revision of a deathbed scene,
> Gloating that he was accurate at last.

If work is no antidote to death, nor a denial of it, death is a powerful stimulus to work. *Get done what you can.*

When I am sick after my operation, not only sore but bonkers the way anaesthesia leaves you, I will write nothing or at least nothing well, but I can fill the days before the operation with work on *Life Work*—and I am determined to write about something besides dying. There's so much I haven't touched on, like my grandfather's daily work, my grandmother Kate's labors—women's work—and ideas from sociologists of work. I have a list of topics to keep me busy. The alternative is tears, appropriate enough but miserable. I keep thinking of Jane, of my mother, of my children and grandchildren. I'm not exactly afraid but I am surely *sad*. Talking with a friend today I said that I was surprised not to feel more frightened, I was surprised to feel pity for Jane more than pity for myself—not that I am without self-pity. Quickly I called myself egotistical, for thinking that my death was the worst thing that could happen to Jane. Then both of us said, at the same time, "Yes, but it is the worst thing that could happen to Jane."

A week from tomorrow John Sutton will remove half my liver. Today is Shakespeare's birthday and my mother's, April 23. She is eighty-nine today. Tonight we will telephone her and tomorrow drive to Connecticut to see her for a couple of days. The beginning of next week I will scramble to finish reading proof, to finish revising *The Museum of Clear Ideas* just in case, to work on new or subsequent poems, and . . . to make arrangements. Arrangements include a long note to Jane, in case I die on the table, about money and manuscripts, possible posthumous essay-collections or collections of poetry. I could die on the table; I could live twenty years. My health is otherwise excellent, blood pressure 130/70, hemoglobin 18. Yesterday I gave a pint of blood, a possible auto-donation . . . but my chances of living five years, Dr. Sutton tells me, are one out of three. The likely sequence, after I recover from this lobectomy, is a gradual return to health accompanied by anxious watching for the next CEA spike. Three spikes and you're out. If cancer comes to my remaining liver, if it comes to my lungs . . . Statistically speaking, a man of my age with my history is likely to die of recurrence, maybe in two or three years. If I buy two or three years, I figure, the years are well bought. On the other hand, if I suffer this operation and die in six months . . . But I speculate; I cannot stop speculating—except when I work.

Letters from friends about manuscript of "Another Elegy" and *The Museum of Clear Ideas* take me back inside my poems and away from my damned liver—but memory of that dark hourglass barbell shape reruns itself on the witless screen. I try to snow it over: *Go away, go away, go away.* Usually I feel calm enough, and when I notice that I am calm I am surprised. But sometimes my hands suddenly go cold. Jane and I hug—standing, sitting, and lying down; sometimes we weep, overcome by the sadness of our eventual absence from each other. Then we dry our eyes and get back to work. Or I talk to my daughter Philippa who is waiting to go into labor, a happy distraction; who seems optimistic and almost convinces me. Or I talk to my son, just thirty-eight and waiting for a new child in a month, who was dark and dour at first but who is now combative; who will, if I require a further more experimental operation, canvas the country for the best treatment, avid and powerful on the telephone. Or I talk to my mother, who last week tortured herself reading in a fifty year old encyclopedia that the liver was untouchable and that metastasis meant prompt death. Or I watch the Boston Celtics (playoffs with Indiana) or the Boston Red Sox, lifting a microphone to dictate to an editor, "This piece is a bit early because . . ." or to a program director, "I won't be able to come . . ." or to a friend far away, "I've got bad news . . ."

Work. Work. Work.

As I recover from this operation, I will be frustrated getting back to work. Letters and manuscripts will accumulate; poems and prose will lie inert, as I lack energy to think or summon language. And I will need to watch out for silliness, inadvertent error, dumb ideas, or even delusion. Is it the anaesthesia? the mania of survival? Last time it was months be-

fore my mind felt normal. How do you watch out for a deluded mind when your only equipment is a deluded mind?

But I continue to obsess, instead of (as I wish) obsessing
to continue.

April 27, late morning, the telephone rings and it is my son-
in-law Jerry: another granddaughter! Abigail and her
mother Philippa are *fine*, and we can see the baby at 2:00
P.M. There is nothing so easily happy as a healthy birth;
happy excitement floods Jane and me. Four granddaughters!
When we see her at Concord Hospital, Philippa is cheerful,
if a bit bruised-looking, and teases me as Jane and I take
turns holding the tiny baby not yet accustomed to air and
light. I had questioned the spelling of their first daughter Allison's name, so Philippa assures me that Abigail is spelled
with two b's. She laughs until she hurts. We drive home, after
setting up a schedule to see Abigail and Philippa over the
next two days, bringing an absorbed excitement with us. It is
essential that my mind stay in the present: Let there be no
daydreams of dancing at Abigail's wedding.

When my first child Andrew was six months old, in early autumn of 1954, we moved to Cambridge where I started three
years in Harvard's Society of Fellows. The Junior Fellowship provided free time: to read, to write, to do whatever I
liked *except* to teach or to undertake formal study. That September, when my wife went back to school to finish her degree, I put my best time into caring for Andrew from 8:00

71

A.M. to 1:00 P.M. six days a week. Oddly enough, I'm not sure that the Senior Fellows who elected us would have disapproved of my first year's project: Junior Fellows were known for following their own noses, for spending three years doing something unexpected. I was elected to write poems—and largely wrote them—but one of my friends, who was a philosopher of aesthetics, spent three years learning to play the piano, then became a philosopher of jurisprudence. Another Junior Fellow devoted most of his energy to being psychoanalyzed. For my first year, I was housefather during the liveliest hours of my day. My wife started Andrew's breakfast and I finished cleaning up by scraping oatmeal from the kitchen ceiling; then I fed him a bottle, gave him his bath, played with him, put him down for a morning nap, made him lunch and another bottle—before my wife, who spent mornings in class and the library, came home and relieved me for the afternoon.

My point, as usual, is work. Afternoons, while my wife strolled Andrew through the streets of Cambridge, I concentrated attention on the page, but even in the morning I worked a little without actually neglecting my baby son. I learned how to feed him a bottle with my left hand crooked around his head that leaned on my left shoulder, to leave my right hand free for a paperback. During baths I played T. S. Eliot on the phonograph. During playpen moments, I sat beside Andrew with a pad and a ballpoint pen, working on lines—some of which were about babies. Once a week, Adrienne Rich came to the apartment for a three hour visit during baby-care. She was pregnant with her first child, and although we talked poetry most of the time, we did not talk only poetry. Like anyone awaiting a first child, Adrienne was nervous about the fragility of an infant, and about the nurturing tasks ahead of her. Twenty-five years later, when so much had happened in our lives, Adrienne and I talked about gender politics in the 1950s; I claimed I wasn't nearly so bad as I might have been. "Don," Adrienne reminded me, "you taught me how to bathe a baby."

In Ann Arbor when I was teaching school, I kept an island of work intact for poetry, separate from teaching, by working on poems each morning from six to eight. For two early hours I grubbed happily at words, before I allowed myself to think of term papers and troubled students. Andrew at three and four years old was an early riser and wanted to play with his father. If I told him to go back to his room and amuse himself, I hurt his feelings; so I invented a scheme: Every morning I wrote him a poem on a subject he assigned. When he requested a poem about "Books," I obliged him:

> I love my books just like a brother.
> I wish that they could read each other.

My endeavors were not only in the form of couplets, but the fewer lines I quote the better: On "Toast," I provided:

> It feels so good to be
> Extremely buttery.

Andrew understood that I sat in my chair each morning "to write poetry"—and when I had written him his daily poem he mounted the stairs to his bedroom apparently satisfied.

Every night I made up stories for him, and later for his sister too. Once Andrew brought me a story himself, telling me that he had a good idea but it was scary. He was going to

73

walk down to the lion store, buy a lion seed, and grow a lion in the window where his mother raised houseplants. Thus I wrote my first children's book, *Andrew the Lion Farmer*, with due credit and a flap picture of father tying son's shoe. Andrew was pleased. As he grew up at school he was proud of my notoriety, and enjoyed the parade of poet-visitors who came to the house—James Wright, Robert Bly, W. D. Snodgrass, Gary Snyder; poetry was obviously what adult males *did*: When he was seven or eight, he asked how old he needed to be, before he went to poetry school.

Andrew went to mathematics school. He completed studies for his Ph.D., except for the dissertation, at which point he decided that, if he were not going to solve unified field theory, he would work in business. He directs quantitative research for a large firm that sells mutual funds, and he has a vocation for fatherhood. Meanwhile, his sister with her two daughters is the best mother I have ever witnessed. All four parents are exemplary. I remind myself that I was not the best father. Although I parted from them little, when I still lived at the house—gone perhaps two nights a month on poetry readings—and although I was home more than most fathers, spending only thirteen or fourteen hours a week at the university, I stayed home to work. My daughter was intensely gregarious, always playing with other children, and we found our intimacies over book-reading and bedtime, which became my precinct. But my son was often as solitary as I had been as an only child. Because I was impatient to write and read, I did not play catch with him as much as I might have done.

When my son was thirteen and my daughter eight, their mother and I separated and two years later divorced. I spent five years between marriages, a wretched time; I stayed in Ann Arbor because of my children, although I could have left for a job at another university or for the poetry chair at the Library of Congress. I spent Mondays after school through supper with both my children; then each of them came overnight once a week. When I was with them then, in those brief hours, I did not work. Still, work was an issue; for a decade when they were in their teens and twenties, their first words and my answer were always the same. They would ask, "What have you been doing?"—and each time I would answer, as if it were something I had just discovered, "*Working!*" It became a joke; we no longer perform the joke.

In the many years since they left Ann Arbor for school (I departed when they did), we were never long apart—and now we live near each other again. I am lucky, since most of my friends have children and grandchildren in Sri Lanka or at least north of Seattle. My Michigan children live in New England—my daughter nearby in New Hampshire, my son outside Boston. I get to roll on the floor with grandchildren, and to tell granddaughters how their great-grandmother Lucy made a clothespin doll for her younger sister at Christmas.

Over the bad years of my life between marriages; or in times of fear and panic; or merely in depression, my mind has always sought comfort in remembering the summers of my childhood that I spent in this house with my grandparents. It was a time and place of affection and security—a high pasture of grass and ferns, surrounded by birches, and it remains in my mind the best idyll of my sixty-four years. I have modelled my late life in this house on my grandparents' as they lived here in work, love, and double-solitude. While I struggle with the beast of my own death, what is more natural than to occupy myself with the tenderness of this recollection?

My grandfather was the model for my adult manhood, more than my father or my father's father. It pleases and amuses me to compare the way I work to the way Wesley Wells did. Comparisons need distance to be useful, and the work is different enough, farmer and writer, but each of us worked or works the whole day at diverse tasks, making an unpredictable living by producing a variety of products: milk, honey, eggs, wood, chicken-flesh, sheep-flesh, calf-flesh, maple syrup, wood for burning and logs for sawing, ice; poems, essays, children's books, textbooks, book reviews; essays on New Hampshire, baseball, and poetry; short stories, plays, and an essay-book on work.

In 1902, when Ben Keneston was seventy-six and running the farm with hired help, Wesley married Kate and moved in—to help run the farm. Insofar as Ben acknowledged the possibility of death, he knew that the farm would endure through his daughter and his daughter's husband. Wesley worked with Ben until Ben's death in 1914, and he never complained of the arrangement in all the years when he told me stories—but I think that it must have been wretched to work with his father-in-law as boss. One story that my mother tells—to illustrate her grandfather's spunkiness up to his death—draws the picture. When Ben was dying of old age at eighty-eight, Wesley pulled into the dooryard with hay loaded onto the hayrack and stopped by the kitchen door before urging the horse up hill to the barn. My mother remembers her grandfather Ben charging out of bed, wearing a red flannel nightgown on a warm summer afternoon, to stick his hand into the hay and make sure it was dry enough.

Wesley had farmed with him for twelve years; Wesley was thirty-seven years old—and his father-in-law/boss didn't grant him sense enough to avoid bringing damp hay to the barn; damp hay was known to cause fires.

Ben's daughter my grandmother in her own nineties still called him Papa ("puppuh"). Kate would change nothing in the house—she would not add a new register to heat an upstairs bedroom, or cut a new door for convenience, or block off an old useless one—because the house remained her father's place; it would stay the way it had suited him. In the early 1980s, five years after Kate's death, when Jane and I added a room and made other structural changes, an annoyed ghost closed doors on us locking us out of the house. Was it her father? Was it Kate's outraged spirit defending her father's house?

My grandfather loved Ben, as his stories made clear, whether or not Ben was a difficult boss. It was Wesley's temperament not to complain—as it was his temperament to show affection. The reader must feel skeptical, like my friend who asks me, "Wasn't there *anything* wrong with him? Was he *perfect*?" Doubtless, I think *yes*, he was perfect. But also I think: Is it blameless never to blame? Maybe I should complain that he never complained; maybe he was accepting to the point of passivity. My grandmother and he played a continual game, like the games all married people play who endure and celebrate decades; the game supports my grudging notion about his imperfection. As they hugged and mumbled together, her tone was always mildly aggrieved while his was always penitent, always promising to do better. (Kate's grievance might be Wesley's failure to wear his cap on a cool dewy morning.) In the economy of their affection, he was always the suitor, she always the reluctant pursued. Possibly Wesley tolerated Ben's bossiness because Wesley enjoyed being bossed.

When Ben died, the small mixed farms of the valley still prospered; but soon the agricultural depression set in—a decade before the crash. By 1918 the little farms of New Hampshire—assembling their livings from cattle, sheep, poultry, sugar, and timber—were done for; by now they are gone. My grandfather kept his enterprise going until 1950; so did many other old men, farming the old way, often alone, in a twilight of the farm culture north of Boston.

In the winter Wesley chopped cordwood on the mountain.

In two or three weeks, I hope to pick up my story again. Today is 30 April 1992, 5:30 A.M., and I must telephone the hospital at 8:30 to learn my time of admission. This afternoon they will dye, photograph, and angio-invade my liver in preparation for tomorrow's lobectomy. May Day. *M'aidez.* In the past week I've done little on *Life Work* because I've been working so much. I've made late discriminations for *The Museum of Clear Ideas*; and—what I didn't know I would do—I've cobbled together the manuscript of a further putative collection to take to the hospital with me, to scribble at, tonight and tomorrow morning—a collection complete with notes for Jane about editing for posthumous publication.

And there've been one or two other things: answering mail with drastic postcards, answering the damned telephone to calm down my friends, conspiring about the NEA meeting that begins today . . . and visiting Abigail Smith.

Last night we brought supper to Philippa and Jerry after she came home from the hospital with Abigail. We congratulated Abigail's three-year-old sister Allison dressed in pink.

Meantime when I dash to the Wilmot library to return books, a neighbor is brave enough to meet my eyes. Angelo at the post office turns pale. Oh, it's a burden for us *morituri*, the way we frighten everybody! Jane has the best story. In Franklin she bumped into Herbert Buckingham the lawyer, as I will call him, who gossips about ideas whenever we meet but who is possibly (in the argot of Carlton Fisk) "dumb as a stick." Herbert casually asks Jane after our health; Jane answers him. With a musing, faraway look in his eyes, he mumbles to Jane, "I never did get to know Don, the way I wanted to."

In the winter Wesley chopped cordwood on the mountain.

It is two and a half weeks later, and I have been home from the hospital for a week. Dr. Sutton removed the big half of my liver, the right lobe, containing all discernible carcinoma. Two days in ICU, two days on the respirator, eight tubes or shunts or IVs or catheters dribbling me away or dripping into me; twelve days in the hospital. When I came home I slept fourteen hours. After three days I started glancing at poems again; I began to answer my mail; today, I pick up *Life Work*.

In my vision, I see Wesley working alone for decades. (I feel calm as I watch him, in my mind's eye, go about his quiet and methodical business.) My mother born in 1903 was followed by Caroline in 1905 and Nan in 1911; Kate wanted for no companionship in the kitchen until Nan went off to college, but Wesley worked mostly alone. Cutting wood in January was the hardest chore of the year. He milked early, ate breakfast, and climbed Ragged with an axe and a lunchpail. All day his axe wedged chunks of hardwood onto snow—ash and maple, oak and elm—the shock and shudder of steel blows aching along his forearms into his shoulders. Because this work was routine, it was endurable though strenuous; keeping a steady pace, he worked past soreness. Sweat froze on his forehead when he stopped to catch his breath. When he chopped down a tree he cut off the branches and cut the burnable trunk and the greater branches into four-foot lengths for transport. He took one break, to eat his lunch, and finished as the afternoon finished. Then he walked down Ragged's icy hill to the relative warmth of milking wedged between Holstein bodies.

When I was twelve and thirteen I heard these stories while we hayed together. Incessantly he remembered things to tell me, often tales of the prodigies or pains of work, told without a whining noise. Over the years, I have often testified to the pleasure I took in his company; as I turn old I think of the pleasure he took in mine—a young male of the family for whom he could describe the journey of a long life, telling about climbing Ragged before dawn in January with an axe and a lunchpail. Later in the winter he drove an ox up hill pulling a sledge, loaded up the cordwood and brought it down for sawing, splitting, drying, and stacking in the woodshed next summer for the winter to follow. After woodchopping, probably the next most difficult task of the year was carting ice from Eagle Pond to store in the icehouse behind the tie-up's watering trough. Neighbors worked together taking ice from the pond, often in February when the ice was two feet thick. First, they scraped snow off, then with horse-drawn cutters scraped long lines onto ice, back and forth, making a checkerboard of ruts, then split the ice into great oblong chunks, then floated ice-slabs to shore, making watery channels for more slabs. Ice-farming, hazards were the cold and the wet, slipping into the freezing water, even drowning dragged down by heavy winter clothes.

Oxen sledged the great oblongs to each farmer's ice-shed—Charley Whittemore was one who worked with Wesley at Eagle Pond—where they packed the slabs under sawdust to last through summer and Indian summer. Every day all summer Wesley brought a new chunk down for the icebox in the shed—Kate's territory—a luminous cube of Eagle Pond slung over his shoulder grappled by iron tongs. Every night another slab floated in a tank beside the milk can from the afternoon milking, keeping milk fresh overnight for the truck that came at dawn.

Everything Wesley did fit into the economy of the farm's year, and most of his work like ice-farming existed for the production of milk. Yet milk paid poorly: Often the monthly milkcheck from H. P. Hood & Sons was less than twenty dollars, and it was good that there were other sources of income. In March, he tapped the sugar maple trees, walking all day in the woods to pound little spigots into the trunks, and to set sapbuckets to catch the drips. Every day he walked through his sweet forest wearing a wooden yoke, like an ox's only smaller, that dangled great pails from each end. He filled the pails with drips from every tree, then emptied them into a tank that an ox pulled to a pipe that gravity-fed downhill to the holding tank of the saphouse.

For making syrup and sugar Wesley needed help, and when he needed help Freeman Morrison supplied it. Freeman—I call him Washington Woodward in *String too Short to be Saved*; in *The Man Who Lived Alone* he lacks a name—

lived alone in his hermit's shack, as dark and cramped as a cave, off New Canada Road three miles north on Ragged. He was my grandmother's cousin, who grew up with her almost like an older brother when Freeman's family was burned out. Freeman loved Wesley as much as he loved Kate. Because he was a night owl, his task in sugaring time was to boil the sap all night, or day and night since he wasn't partial to sleep if there was work to do.

In the farm's year spring was busy, not painful like winter but varied in its chores and lengthy. Lambs and calves were born, increase of Jacob's flock, and the farmer played midwife. In April Wesley sheared the sheep, sometimes with vagrant professional help. The sale of wool and lambs paid the farm's taxes. Some years my grandfather like many citizens paid part of his taxes in kind by working on town roads. Freeman, who practiced an almost-cashless economy, hauled hardpan by oxcart and wheelbarrow to fill washed-out places on dirt roads. Wesley rolled snow on the road that passes the farm. The snow roller, pulled by horses or oxen, looked like the fat wheel at the front of a steamroller, a cart's width; it packed the snow down so that horses could draw their sleighs across it.

In spring Wesley manured his fields, carting the sweet deep accumulation of Holstein manure to spread where the garden grew and where the cattle's fieldcorn would grow eight feet tall by late August. Anything left over went on the home hayfields that rotated with cornfields. Twice a day all year long he hoed the manure out of the tie-up, lifting with his hoe a leather-hinged board that opened a long aperture to the manure pile underneath. Now he loaded five or eight times a day the manure cart that he used only two weeks a year—it was otherwise parked unused in the barn beside its source—shoveling it full and spreading the manure by tilting the cart's bed. Then he planted fieldcorn and vegetables, harrowed, and weeded. Then he hayed.

Each day was a complex of tasks, with milking at the two portals of the day. Kate cared for the hens and harvested the eggs and kept as busy all day into the night as Wesley did. Kate worked on the huge garden also, planting and weeding with Wesley. When it came time for setting poles to raise Kentucky Wonders, Freeman walked down the mountain to help. I forgot to say—

(I forget things; and there are surely chores I never knew of, as I walked in Hamden, Connecticut, to and from Spring Glen Grammar School, melancholy in the suburbs, thinking of my grandparents in New Hampshire, missing the farm)—

I forgot to mention the spring day when the chicks arrived, when Henry Powers's West Andover post office turned into a cheep-house as cardboard boxes arrived in the mail from the chick factories. Wesley carried cardboard cartons home, boxes singing like a field of crickets, and opened them in the shed. Shipped as eggs, the chicks cracked their shells open on the journey, and always a few whole eggs remained, failures, and maybe one or two stiff little yellow birds lay dead, but mostly each box strutted with fifty or a hundred downy miniature chickens. When they were big enough and the nights were warm, the chicks crossed the road to the chicken yard and the coop where they slept, protected from skunk and fox. When I came to the farm in summer they were my task: I fed them grain and brought them water twice a day. By the end of the summer the females were turning into pullets, though their little eggs had not started, and young roosters went off by truck for slaughter. Pullets became hens in the henhouse, producing eggs that Kate swapped at Henry's for coffee and salt, or that Kate collected in egg cartons in the toolshed for the Boston eggman to pick up every two weeks, fresh eggs. As the old hens slowed their egg production and took to setting, each took her turn in the kettle. There was a chopping block in the sheepyard near the henhouse with a hatchet stuck into it. Once a year this hatchet divested the lambs of their tails; once in a lifetime each hen, a reward for faithful service, lost her head to hatchet and chopping block. Then my grandmother plucked her feathers and eviscerated her on the porch—cats gathered for portions of hen—and the carcass boiled for hours (these creatures were old, tough, muscled, and gamey) to provide us fricassee. Thus everything fit. More and more it fit into poverty.

These days are short, as I sleep ten or twelve hours. When I feel pain I take pills that make me sleepy. But I recover more mental energy every day, and I need no longer read John Le Carré but return to Pepys, Montaigne, Browning, and St. Paul. When I began writing last week, I could manage only a page at a go. Now I can go four pages, visiting again the high pasture of forty years ago.

In the mixed farm's economy there were cash crops harvested once a year—syrup; sheep's wool; lambs; young roosters; bull calves for the butcher—and all year there was milk for cash and eggs for barter. On the other hand, the vegetable garden provided food directly—without conversion into the decimals of cash, then reconversion into tins—all year long. Kate and Wesley never bought a vegetable. A generation or two earlier, before Sears and the division of labor made the task superfluous, farmers never bought clothes. They grew and made their clothes: out of flax laboriously converted into linen, spun and woven; out of sheep's wool washed and carded and spun and woven. By my grandparents' times the farm economy had moved toward the abstractions of finance: Syrup converted into a money order mailed itself to Sears for the cotton that did not grow in New Hampshire; syrup converted came back as overalls, long underwear, nightshirts, blue workshirts, and yards of material for dresses and aprons.

The mixed farm's economy gradually failed during the long shift from the old cashless farmlife (sometimes called subsistence farming) to the money-economy that the railroad engendered when it provided markets for milk.

My grandfather had his doubts about the cow-economy. Sheep take little work compared to cattle; you don't milk them and they'll eat rough forage. Holsteins are finicky; Holsteins prefer millet or clover to good honest hay. Sometimes while I hayed with him my grandfather would speculate: If he were a young man now he'd concentrate on sheep. He described the barn he would build for his sheep, and the fences he would make, and the reservoir he would fashion from concrete on the hill over the house against fire. (He was always frightened of fire.) He was daydreaming that I might follow him at the farm.

When we talked about his year's work, I was helping my grandfather hay in the summers of the 1940s; briefly he had a companion for his labors. In those summers my grandmother brought me black coffee at six in my bedroom—the same room I write in now, fifty years later—and I set to work, making poems and stories or reading books with the notion of a literary vocation. I took an early break, feeding chickens, while my grandfather milked. At the evening milking, I sat on a three-legged stool in the tie-up while he milked telling me stories and reciting poems. I learned to milk slowly and inefficiently; he always finished my cow, last strokes to strip the udder.

After the morning milking my grandfather's work was a series of chores on a list he never wrote down: He fed the horse and checked out the vegetable garden, weeding until the sun dried dew off the hay. Then he took his scythe down from the crotch of the dooryard maple, where it hung overnight, and sharpened it with a blue whetstone he carried in the back pocket of his overalls, his hand moving so quickly that it blurred, switching the whetstone at each scrape from one edge of the scythe to the other, an action I duplicated ten times more slowly. Then he set off with Riley on the mowing machine—sitting in the metal scoop of its seat, his scythe mounted over his shoulder—for the field he would cut this morning.

My grandfather taught me scythe mowing, which is a rhythmic motion like dancing or lovemaking. It is a studious sweeping crescent in which the trick is to keep the heel (where blade joins snath) close to the ground, an angle that tilts the scythe point-up, preventing it from catching in the ground. I no longer mow with a scythe—a certain recipe for lower-back muscle spasms—but remember it the way the body remembers weights and leanings: riding a bicycle, skiing, casting flies. Finding a meter, one abandons oneself to the swing of it; one surrenders oneself to the guidance of object and task, where worker and work are one: There is something ecstatic about mowing with a scythe.

Wesley cut most of his hay with Riley's help, the mowing machine clacketing beside him, cutting swaths of hayfield up and down and around. Then he paused, resting Riley in the shade, climbed down from his iron perch, fetched his scythe where it hung in another tree crotch, and trimmed around rocks, trees, or at the field's edge where Riley could not mow for fear of snagging or snapping a steel tooth against rock or wire. Farmers no longer trim fields. The old trimming was uneconomic—an hour of hand-cutting produced seventeen cents worth of hay—but it wasn't done for economic reasons; nothing was done for economic reasons. Things were done because it was the way to do them, an aesthetic of work, old habits bespeaking clarity and right angles, resolution and conclusiveness.

After a morning of cutting, my grandfather unhitched Riley from the mowing machine, or drove him home, pulling the machine, if the field was done. He watered and grained Riley, ate dinner and took a ten-minute nap on the living room's wicker sofa. Then he hitched Riley to the rake, twice as wide as the mowing machine, with its curved metal tines that lifted and lowered by a lever beside the metal seat. My grandfather raked the hay into long wavery rows, then pulled the rows into small stacks by tugging the row on top of itself. When the field was spotted with piles of hay, he switched Riley from rake to rack, backing the old horse between the shafts of the homemade hayrack. The shafts were sapling poles with the bark off, homemade hardware added. (Like most farmers, Wesley kept his own forge; the shop stood near the saphouse, where he or Freeman made or repaired the farm's iron hinges and implements; beside the forge was a lathe for turning wood.) The rack's floor was pine planks, two wells cut in the flooring up front for the great wheels to turn into—wooden wheels with iron rims. From the edge of the flooring spokes leaned up-and-outward, three feet long and an inch thick with bark still on them, rising to split pole rails that formed a long narrow rectangle holding the hay in.

Loading the hayrack by himself had to be a fiddle. When I

worked with him, we could fit three jobs—pitching on, loading, raking after—into two bodies; it was best when Anson the hired-man worked with us, some wartime summers, when three bodies divided the three chores. This was the old way of haying—no baler, no bales—when one worker with a pitchfork lifted a forkful to another with a pitchfork on top of the rack, who loaded the hay, tucking it here and there with the fork and treading it down; the loader's trick was to knit the hay together so that it would not tumble apart on the journey home, to tuck and tread the forkfuls as if weaving a basket, then at home in the barn to unpack the hay and fork it into a hayloft: putting it together, taking it apart. Meantime the third partner, least skilled, pulled a wide wooden bullrake over ground where the stacks had been, cleaning and tidying, following the wagon to the next stack, swinging the bullrake up to deposit its fringe of hay on the next stack.

Pitching, loading, and raking after. I can see the three of us working in 1942—fifty years gone, as I write—a classic frieze: My grandfather at sixty-seven—dark-skinned with sun, strong and tall, vigorous in his overalls and blue shirt with the sleeves rolled up, wearing a blue cloth cap—stands by the haystack and plunges his pitchfork in, turns it slightly to catch as if setting the hook in a pickerel's mouth, lifts, balances, and swings it over his head to land at Anson's feet. Halfwit or not, Anson knew about loading hay; he tucked and treaded, tucked and treaded. Meantime I pulled the great rake—four feet wide with tines a foot long and a gracefully curved handle—gathering fugitive strands of hay, taking care to avoid catching a tine in a woodchuck hole and snapping it off. Pitchforks and bullrakes were the antique implements of haying that the Director of the Historical

Museum of Hokkaido outside Sapporo showed us behind glass cases in 1986.

When he hayed alone Wesley heaved forkfuls in, then climbed up to load, then climbed down to rake and lead Riley to another haymow. When the two of us hayed we traded off, one of us loading and the other doubling to pitch on and rake after. Usually I loaded, standing on top of the hay in a good sweat, catching the breeze, watching my grandfather's practiced rhythm with the fork: *plunge in, turn, heave, swing, shake loose, and back for more.*

Each day is a little longer and lighter, but there are setbacks: a night I cannot sleep; or a new pain in a new place, bringing back the fear of imminent death: I live at the point of anxiety, familiar enough, when a toe cramp fosters speculation about toe cancer. Every day is a seesaw of hope and despair. When I am sore and tired discouragement settles over me like smog over Los Angeles. I suppose I will get better; but then I will be sick again, then die. Once a day I weep and Jane joins me, hugging and weeping. Once a day she rubs down my thin slack body, willing health to it with her strong and benignant fingers.

Freeman Morrison was a free-lancer, one of so many independent old men who holed up in shacks all over New England. As I remember the story, during the Great War he worked in a factory for a salary; I cannot accommodate the notion that he kept regular hours for a regular stipend because in the years I knew him he was the ultimate antinomian. He was a good roofer and a night owl: He set lanterns in trees and on ridgepoles and roofed by night. He canned huge quantities of peas and beans, corn and tomatoes, beets and carrots—and ate one deer and one woodchuck every year. He lived almost entirely without cash, contriving work to please himself by moving rocks from place to place, by grafting apple trees, by raising an ox for a pet. He worked on the road to pay his taxes. When my mother and Caroline attended Bates College in the 1920s, occasionally they received a note from Freeman with a nickel wrapped up inside. Have a treat.

Freeman was intelligent, garrulous, diligent, conservative, inventive, and eccentric. He hated to feel beholden, but worked with (not for) Wesley and Kate because he loved them. He worked with assiduousness compounded by shrewdness. In 1938 the hurricane left the gravity-well—that watered not only the kitchen but the troughs for cattle and sheep—thick with debris, too sluggish to flow and too riley to drink. My grandfather could not handle it himself, with everything else he had to do after the hurricane, so he hired McIndoe the plumber to come up from Andover with two handpumps and some strong backs. They worked all day and couldn't get rid of the riley sludge; runoff from the deluge kept ahead of them. So Kate suggested Freeman, sent him a penny postcard to his camp on Ragged, and the next evening Freeman walked down to the farm. Then he climbed up hill with a lantern, two boiled eggs, a shovel, and three sap-buckets. When Wesley ascended in the dawn with a bacon sandwich, Freeman was clambering out of the clean well, clear water filling it, his lantern still lit in the brightening dawn.

Upstairs in this house, the south bedroom of the original

Cape is "Freeman's room," where he stayed as a boy. He paneled the room, and arranged a pulley for the trapdoor in the ceiling that went up-attic. In Freeman's room we still keep some of the things he collected and kept there in his old age (Kate outlived him) because his camp was so crowded: clocks, calendars, a hornets' nest, and his old trunk, round-topped like a pirate's chest: Here we find slates that Freeman used at school, chalk, fancy mittens and socks he never wore, a cube of dried purple ink, an inkwell, a pen, and diaries from the 1880s well into the twentieth century; here Freeman kept his financial records, receipts for twenty-five cents and half a dollar—and notes of work done:

worked in stable all day, went down and got my stove in evening, put part of it upstairs in my room and the rest of it up to the shop . . . worked in woods all day chopping wood and cutting brush . . . put up eight quart cans of pears in evening.

. . . worked on plants a while then worked in shop repairing stoves in forenoon; worked in woods in afternoon chopping wood. There was a prayer meeting at Ben's tonight. Fred Peasley leader.

. . . worked in woods chopping all day . . .

. . . worked in well forenoon and got in four loads of corn in afternoon. Put rest of wood into the schoolhouse shed.

. . . worked in well all day laying stone. Jammed my finger badly.

. . . worked in well all day, laying stone.

. . . took care of the corn then filed saw. Went down and set up stove for S. Dudley. Fixed the boards on the end of barn. Then went over and done Ed Downes chores. (Washed out gun at noontime.)

. . . stayed over to Ed's last night. This morning done all

of his chores, then went out through Gales Woods and looked it over. Then came home . . .

These are Freeman's lists, the accounting of each day by chores accomplished: Acts of the Apostles of Work.

Freud loved work. At the prime of his life in Vienna, he was said to live by the clock. Compulsiveness? Anyone who loves accomplishment lives by the clock and the list. Freud's biographer Peter Gay described his workday in his fifties. He went to bed at one in the morning, rose at seven, saw analytic patients from eight to twelve, dined with his family at one, then walked in the city—where he bought cigars, where he did errands like delivering proof—and at three began appointments again. Sometimes he saw patients until nine at night. Supper. Then maybe a card game, maybe another walk with his wife to a cafe, then reading and writing and editing. Freud liked riding horses—and was known to conduct an analysis with a patient riding alongside him. His weekends varied but remained thick with his cherished work. He lectured every Saturday from five to seven, then played cards with a friend. Sunday mornings he visited his mother; Sunday afternoons he wrote letters.

When he grew old and ill he did not change his mind about work; his physical and political circumstances altered, you might say, with the double advent of jaw-cancer and Hitler. He escaped Vienna at the last minute for England but brought his cancer with him, and the prosthesis which made eating and talking possible but which caused him continual pain. In England he wrote the great tragic late work, including *Civilization and Its Discontents*, in which "discontent" is understatement (or magical euphemism) like the surgeon's "discomfort." In his last books, Freud wrote of the wretchedness, torture, and misery fundamental to civilized human life. A major palliative is work: "One gains the most if one can sufficiently heighten the yield of pleasure from the sources of psychical and intellectual work." "A satisfaction of this kind, such as an artist's joy in creating, in giving his phantasies body, or a scientist's in solving problems or discovering truths, has a special quality. . . ." D. H. Lawrence spoke of the task to expand human consciousness, which Freud took upon himself: "Where id was let there ego be."

But, of course, "the weak point of this method [artist's or scientist's] is that it is not applicable generally: it is accessible to only a few people. It presupposes the possession of special dispositions and gifts which are far from being common to any practical degree. And even to the few who do possess them, this method cannot give complete protection from suffering. It creates no impenetrable armor against the arrows of fortune, . . ." Then Freud allows himself the mildest allusion to his own suffering: "[this method] habitually fails when the source of suffering is a person's own body."

Wesley and Kate harvested vegetables all summer long—peas and beans, carrots and greens, whatever was ripe—first to eat at the daily table and then to preserve. Prodigies of canning occupied my grandmother's July and August kitchen. Golden Bantam corn heaped the table every night in August; tomatoes raw and cooked sat beside them, and other tomatoes filled rows of Ball jars. Late summer the root vegetables descended to the dirt-floored root cellar.

As summer heightened, the cattle wandered further off

each day in search of newer and sweeter grass, or to avoid the plaguy flies. Now to his workday of milking and haying my grandfather added a long hike every afternoon to find and fetch the herd. When they had been out all night they never wandered so far, but clustered for the morning's milking at the barn-end of the pasture, their swollen udders dripping. However, at four in the afternoon they seldom left the pleasures of pasturing to return to the barn. He knew the forest places where they were likely to be, but these sweet clearings were not adjacent. He climbed and called, a long piercing call of "Ke-bosh, ke-bosh, ke-bo-o-o-o-sh," which I assume derived from "Come, Bossie." (Maybe not; the sheep-call was "Ke-day," which I can connect with nothing.) He listened for one stroke of a cowbell. When finally he found the cattle nosing a bosky dell with white drops oozing out of them, they turned and filed to the barn.

Only one device induced them to return to the barn on their own: reward. Every year my grandfather grew, on a home field, an especially tasty acre: maybe millet or a sweet grass he called "Hungarian." After haying, before milking— with no cows visible—he would scythe-mow a heaping wheelbarrow-load of special grass and stow a good swatch in each cow's feeding trough, which they would find waiting for them on their tardy return. A few days of this treat—this grass must have tasted like strawberry-rhubarb pie—and the cattle would file down the hill by three-thirty or four, eager for treats.

One September polio boiled from the Connecticut beaches through city to suburb; schools delayed opening, and I stayed longer on the farm, long enough to see the culmination of the summer's work in the harvest of fieldcorn and its translation into ensilage. My grandfather cut his three acres of fieldcorn behind Riley pulling the mowing machine: thick-stemmed grass. We stacked it into the hayrack and piled it in front of the barn like skinny green cordwood eight feet long. Then a crew of three men with a gasoline-driven machine set up near the silo, which was just inside the barn door, and chopped the long cornstalks and blades and ears into smithereens and blew them into the silo where my grandfather all winter would serve them each day like vitamins to barn-bound cattle.

The cattle continued to graze while there was green grass to eat. While hay still grew my grandfather hayed. Then in autumn came a relatively calm time in the farm's work year— before harsh January and its logging on the hill. Wesley brought in the sheep, and lambs went off in the butcher's truck as the bull calves did. He patrolled his fences, sheep pasture and cow pasture, rolling stones or cutting brush or nailing wire where he spied holes. Summer's work was always interrupted by errant sheep who, for all their stupidity, were quick to find and file through any gap. Cattle were less apt to wander; in the pursuit of sweet grass they filed up-mountain instead of investigating perimeters. One summer his two heifers—tucked away in a special pasture by themselves to feed while they bulked out before breeding—broke loose and went wild. We spent a whole day chasing them.

There were other autumn chores: repairing equipment and storing it for winter; picking apples to barrel the keepers in the cellar for winter's pies; pressing cider from bruised or imperfect apples to make vinegar, hoeing out potatoes and storing them with other roots. Then it was time to fix the house for winter, to rake leaves against the foundations all around the house and to cut spruce boughs, laying them over the leaves to keep the leaves in place. When the first snow came Wesley shoveled it over leaves and spruce to tuck the house up for winter. And there was wood to cut into stove-length pieces, to split and stack in the woodshed. The sleighs and sledges were ready. Then there was Christmas, then January and cutting cordwood for another winter—entering again upon the year and the year's work.

This life was not de Crevecoeur's paradise. The farm produced little money, and my grandfather wore my father's old hand-me-downs; everywhere rags of poverty flourished like skunkweed. Still, my grandparents appeared to enjoy their work, which did not extend human consciousness but occupied or absorbed it. Elsewhere there were miserable farmers who should not have been farmers, who lacked the vocation for it and never got their work done, or did it so late that it failed: Green wood burns badly; hay without nutriment makes poor milk. The old people spoke of feckless farmers not with contempt for laziness but in hushed and nervous tones as if they spoke of an illness. If work was life, working badly was a wasting disease.

Although their work was endless, I never heard my grandparents complain about it or whine. Work was *there* like Mt. Everest. I speak of both my grandparents, although I've written so far about Wesley: Kate worked as much or more than he did. I speak of him first because—as I was ten and twelve and fourteen—he was my model, my companion, my tale-teller, my poem-reciter, my source or entrance into the great cavern of old time: the Civil War, the blizzard of '88, the Boston and Maine controlling the New Hampshire legislature. (In politics, his daily New Deal rant converted me from the businessman Republicanism of my father and my father's father.) But as I loved him and his work, I also lived in the house of Kate's work and affection. I dwelt summers within the little estate they made, out of love and work together.

This estate depended on women's work. When I spoke earlier of gardening, canning, and egg-harvesting, I touched on Kate's work—because they collaborated on these tasks—but to a large extent they ruled separate domains. He was lord of barn and outdoors, of animals and hay; she was empress of kitchen, Glenwood Range, and house, wholly in charge of food, clothing, preservation, cleanliness, and comfort. Kate was strong, stout, controlling, and *tireless*: Oh,

> Man may work from sun to sun
> But woman's work is never done.

Wesley worked from sun to sun, but he *did* stop working: He read the *Boston Post*, fuming over Republicans and grinning over Ted Williams; on Sundays, and frequently in the evening after supper and shutting up the hens, before Gabriel Heatter with bread and milk at nine o'clock, he sat reading novels—maybe forty-five minutes of the same novel over again: *David Harum*, or anything by Joe Lincoln, or by Grace Livingston Hill or Kathleen Norris. (He once let me know that high society folks lacked morals.) At Christmas he received one or two of these novels, Sears catalog hardback reprints at sixty-nine cents. He sat in the Morris chair by the light set on the round table, his face working with response, and if the book was a Joe Lincoln, he laughed every ninety seconds.

Kate didn't read. On Sundays she might read Scripture, and once a week she glanced through the *Franklin Transcript* that carried local news and obituaries—but this straight-A student from Franklin High School never read a book. She

97

didn't *want* to read a book; she had better things to do. Although she was Sabbatarian, her code would have allowed her to read on Sunday, even to read fiction. (My father and I could not play catch with a baseball on a Sunday; we could not play croquet or badminton; we could not listen to baseball games on the radio. My grandfather worked at his animal chores, maybe four hours, because cows were unsabbatarian.) Even on Sunday Kate sat without reading as her mind worked things over; she daydreamed, she planned. She allowed herself a little handwork—making potholders or aprons, crocheting lace for handkerchiefs—providing it was for sale at the Church fair.

On weeknights she sewed or darned while Wesley read, and her work was never done. She darned socks and stitched torn shirts and underwear. If her basket of repair-work was empty, then she knitted mittens for winter, or made socks, or did more fancywork, crocheting and tatting. It kept her hands busy, a form of recreation, and while she worked she kept on thinking; sometimes her lips formed words. Every five or ten minutes she would say something out loud— while my grandfather and I were reading—and we could follow the geography of her thought. "It *does* seem to rain a lot in Connecticut," she would say, and I would know that she was remembering a postcard from my mother. ("Mmm," my grandfather and I would respond in chorus.) "Do you suppose Caroline will teach social studies after all?"—and she was thinking of my aunt who filled in for a friend at a Massachusetts high school.

Kate never kept lists, she just kept moving. At 5:00 A.M., Wesley started the fire in the Glenwood kitchen range, three hundred sixty-five days a year, rumbling a tin can full of kerosene over sticks assembled in the firebox. Maybe Wesley stuck the kettle over the fire, starting the process of Kate's dripped coffee, strongest in the universe, but thereafter Kate tended the range all day long, even in hot summer—for breakfast and noontime dinner, for pies and canning. (On the hottest days we took our supper cold.) Wesley stacked wood in the woodbox by the stove but Kate split wood herself when she needed a hot fire, and all day she cared for the range's fire as she once cared for babies, not only in feeding but in adjusting the poise of temperature by louvres and drafts and placement of pots on hot surfaces, exercising without consciousness ten thousand acquired skills.

Monday she rolled the great washing machine from the shed to the kitchen, opening up the set tubs and grinding the week's clothing through the wringer, water boiling on the Glenwood and Kate's face red and shiny until sheets and shirts hung flapping on the clothesline secured by gray clothespins. Tuesday she ironed, using a sequence of flat-irons that heated on the Glenwood's hottest places. She picked them up in turn by a universal wooden handle, and returned each for reheating when she exhausted its usable heat. Wednesday baking? Say Wednesday and Saturday baking, when my mother was a girl, twenty loaves of bread a week (but later you could buy soft bread already sliced in greased paper, that never went stale—white airy bread, a wonder as they called it) and pies by the half-dozen: rhubarb in spring; apple much of the year, pumpkin and mince; strawberry briefly and blueberry always (from canning): pies on the table three meals a day. Every day she cooked with salt pork from the cairn in the cellar, and with homegrown maple syrup and honey, and with vinegar kept in the cellar where she descended for her Ball jars. In summer she sat on the porch snapping Kentucky Wonders, bushels at a time, to cook up with onions, milk, and salt pork or to put into four hundred jars; or she sat on the porch shelling peas, dense green shot thudding like hail into the aluminum kettle. When my mother and her sister were girls, the family of five enlarged with hired men at harvest. After supper Wesley and maybe a hired man would pick bushels of beans or tomatoes or berries, and Kate would sit on the porch with her daughters shelling peas or culling berries or shucking corn for tomorrow's canning or jam-making, and for tomorrow's dinner.

When cooking or preparing paused a little, before the evening of darning or repairs, Kate made clothes, tissue-paper patterns set on the dining-room table cleared of bread, pies, vinegar, syrup, and salt; then the chick-chick-chickle of the treadle-operated sewing machine—there are three in the attic—as Kate sewed dresses and aprons, fancy and plain, coats and blouses and skirts. And she cleaned house, regularly each week and twice a year in special, hauling quilts and mattresses and a dozen hooked rugs outside for shaking and spanking. She emptied chamber pots, killed insects, and set mousetraps. Cats lived in the barn—animals *outside*; people *inside*—though now and again, when rodent infestation became intolerable, one cat gained temporary inside patrol duty. To clean the floors she used mops and brooms, no vacuum cleaner; she dusted, she waxed, and she ended every day by washing the precious hardwood floor of her kitchen. The floors of the other rooms were wide soft pine protected by rugs. The proud hardwood floor of the kitchen darkened every night with Kate's mopping.

Community life made more work. There was cooking for others, for the sick or for potluck, for Church or for Grange. There were meetings of the King's Daughters Sewing Circle, Willing Workers Branch, a devotional program mounted among a dozen women who gathered to sew, each bringing a basket of private work, or cooperating to provide the many hands needed for quilting. Oh, woman's work was never done, or done only on Sundays when Kate sat hatted and coated by the door an hour before Ansel and Edna took us to Church in the Model A, sitting still with her busy hands calm in her lap—the only time all week that her hands were idle—her eyes faraway and her mouth working, thinking . . . of what? I come back, always, to the mysterious inner life of Kate Keneston Wells. With Wesley one knew what he thought because he spoke it. Was Kate thinking of the hymns she would play on the organ, an hour hence? Maybe she thought of her daughters to whom she wrote every day but Sunday, penny postcards often, sometimes letters—news of weather, news of how the hens are laying and of the rain that frustrated haying, news of the illness of old neighbors, news of quarts canned, of curtains washed and put back up; advice of the week ahead: Air out the back chamber, pick beans and can them.

This work that was never done was the work of the house, domain or empire of the woman who provided food, shelter, clothing—for her father Ben, for Lucy, Caroline, and Nan, for Wesley, for expanding and contracting crews of itinerant helpers through haying and harvest, logging and sugaring and sheep-shearing. As with the farmer, the farmwife's daily and yearlong work seldom saw the color of money. Work made food and the clean rooms of health. But as the farmer raised cash by selling sheep's wool, cordwood, eggs, and syrup; or as the smithy made a wagon once a year—so some farmwives added to family income by running a part-time commercial enterprise. My grandmother in her spare time made and sold hats. For a couple of decades the parlor at the front of the old Cape was the millinery shop. In old photographs of this house you can read a sign lettered over the front door: *Millinery*. Kate noted that she and her neighbors lacked a hat store, in an era of spectacular hats. She was good with her hands; now she developed an eye for fashion. Once a year she took the train to Boston—to buy new hats and hat material, and to look at the latest fashions. When my mother was big enough she accompanied her mother on these excursions—all morning chugging south, in midday the noise and roil of the metropolis, a late chug back—and remembers best a Woolworth's with a mile-long counter of penny toys; for a penny you could buy a doll's hot-water bottle that really held water.

When Kate returned she copied the fashionable hats she bought, making new hats from scratch, and set them on wire hat-pedestals in the parlor. Farmwives tied horses outside the house and came to the parlor to shop for millinery. Some bought new; others brought weary old hats that they left for revivification—a new piece of bright ribbon; a little stitching; a bright new cloth rose; an ostrich feather. From time to time, Kate shut up her store, loading it onto the buggy, and became hat peddler to wives isolated on the backroads in the hills. She drove into their yards with her merchandise, sold what she had and took orders. On these hat-selling excursions she developed the reputation of a demon driver. She stood upright in the front of the carriage, laying reins on the horse's back to demand celerity, all five foot two of her; her daughter Caroline remembered when a horse stumbled in a rapid trot and Kate steadied him upright by the force of her tidy powerful body.

By the time I remember—1930s and 1940s—the millinery business was done for, outdistanced by catalogs, by itinerant salesmen driving Fords, and by Chevies that took farmwives to the millinery stores of Franklin or Laconia. Traces of the old trade remain throughout this house, especially the wire hat-pedestals that rise like metal crab grass in the black hole upstairs. (I put the first overhead light into this storage place under the eaves.) When I lived with my grandparents, Kate's direct economic contribution had dwindled to control of the egg concession. Still she worked like my grandfather the sixteen-hour day and the six-day week.

When she was forty-four years old, the United States and the State of New Hampshire, in generous condescension, decided to allow her to vote.

❧

Men and women, in the old farm accommodation, worked equally hard—give or take a farmer's Grace Livingston Hill—and this equality (I will argue) carried weight, import, and impact. There was no female equality outside work, not in property nor in citizenship. Town meeting took place every March: Ben voted, Wesley voted, but the women stayed home.

Power is not democratic, I need hardly acknowledge, even in a democracy. The house was Kate's domain of power, whatever the ownership, whatever the name to which the taxbill was addressed. Power came from work. When she was growing up, Kate had another dream of work and domain. Children of the Protestant churches, from the eighteenth century well into the twentieth, dreamed the romance of foreign missions—a permissible romance of goodness. (By this time, we understand that missions—these medicines of largesse and martyrdom—were wicked tools of empire and oppression; Kate lacked our wisdom.) As a senior in Franklin High School, she was admitted to Baltimore Women's Medical College (the female counterpart of Johns Hopkins) to study for her M.D. and become a medical missionary in Africa or China. All other females of her family became schoolteachers (work) before settling down as farmwives (work) but Kate would practice medicine (work) and spread the gospel (work). Then, her mother fell suddenly ill and died. As far as I can tell—or as far as any of her daughters could tell—Kate changed direction without wavering or doubting for a moment. She took over the house for the bereaved widower Ben and, a few years later, added a husband and started a family, undertaking the women's work that was never done. No one of us—talking with her about her mother and father; about straight A's in Greek, Latin, mathematics and everything else at Franklin; about admission to medical school (she was still proud of her admission, and of her report card, in her nineties)—ever heard a moment's regret or self-pity; I don't think she felt any. I remember Kate's day—her concentration, her dawn-to-dusk labor—from the time she was in her late fifties until she slowed down toward senility at ninety-two and died mindless at ninety-seven—and I do not believe that she resented her life of work, although some friends of mine who never knew her (or her culture) have argued against my conviction. I think she took mild continual pleasure in completing tasks, in numbering the four hundredth Ball jar of Kentucky Wonders, or in the poundage of clothes wrung out and hung on the line. I see her, or I feel her in my memory, *satisfied*—by her competence, by her control, by her powerful regency in her domain. She stands astride Eagle Pond Farm like a short, stout Colossus, a rolling pin in one hand and a spatula in the other, with a fierce and purposeful if distracted look in her eye, her body and mind marching to a tune of the day's work, work, work.

May 28 would be my first appointment with the surgeon after leaving the hospital May 12. I hoped to be allowed to drive. On May 23, Jane's birthday, I was working and napping, napping and working—when the phone rang from Yale–New Haven Hospital. My mother had stopped breathing and turned blue in the emergency room, having used her failing breath to dial 911 and whisper her address. A tube breathed for her now; it looked as if she would survive. Immediately, we began to calculate. If she had been dying we would have gone to her. If she were not dying, we would gather our strength (and Dr. Sutton's permission) to drive to Connecticut the day before the hospital released her, to bring her home and set her up again to live alone, if she could, because living alone in her own house is her remaining life's passion.

The next day in the morning the telephone rang again. Andrew delivered the news that Natalie had given birth to Peter, fifth grandchild and first male, large and redheaded like his father.

Dr. Sutton allowed me to drive. Yale–New Haven kept my mother until June 1. On Sunday, May 31, we drove to Connecticut by way of Abigail in Concord, New Hampshire, and Peter in Belmont, Massachusetts—Jane and I driving by turns—and the next morning we brought my mother back to the house on Ardmore Street, and mother and I traded respirator-stories. I brought her news of great-grandchildren, especially the new advent of a boy destined to be coddled by four elder sisters and first cousins. Home again and happy, my mother worked like crazy—paying bills in the morning, arranging her new medicines after lunch, in the afternoon preparing and cooking string beans the way she loves them. We would stay a week, and go home on Monday, the eighth of June.

This morning I began a new longish poem called "The Daughters of Edward D. Boit" as I sat tired and sore in the Ardmore Street house where we moved when I was seven in 1936, and where I wrote my first poem in 1940. The poem gives off a posthumous odor.

On the one hand there was the rhyme that told us that women's work was never done. On the other hand, in mid-nineteenth-century industrial and imperialist England, Charles Kingsley wrote, "For men must work, and women must weep." He wrote as neurasthenia became epidemic among middle-class Victorian females.

As everyone knows, in the last decade or so American families have come to require a double income—and it is the norm for women to work at regular jobs outside the house. It is assumed by right-wing defenders of family values that women never worked as they work now. Although the present circumstances of women's work differ from the old conditions, women have almost always worked: For most social classes, the era of forced leisure for women was brief, insofar as it existed, and in all the history of men's brutality to women, men have never punished women so much as when—in city and suburb, at different historical moments according to social class, from the eighteenth century into the twentieth—men removed from women the necessity or convention of work equal in quantity and importance to men's work.

Beginning as early as the late eighteenth century, growing

widespread in Victorian times and increasing through much of the twentieth century, husbands and fathers demanded that wives and daughters be idle and decorative, proof of male power and economic success. The requirement of idleness, disguised as benignity, was a massive and malignant assault.

Oh, a Victorian housewife of means, not allowed to become a doctor or a marketing executive, might find herself executive nonetheless—managing a squad of nannies as well as a platoon of housemaids, cooks, gardeners, laundresses, grooms, and coachmen. But of course the majority of our ancestors were the laundresses, grooms, cooks, teachers, nannies, gardeners, and coachmen; others were subsistence farmers or hired hands in a society still largely agricultural—and in the work of an agricultural society, women worked as much as men did.

Contrast, with laundresses and farmwives, the lawyer's daughter in 1919 or the businessman's wife in 1884. With heroic exceptions, these women were denied not only the vote but the dignity of utility. They were permitted the vapors and forbidden education; they could not labor except for Lady Bountiful's volunteering; they could not sew shirts or cook stews; they were allowed to make lace, play piano, paint watercolors, and pour tea.

When Emile Durkheim wrote the *Division of Labor* a century ago, he developed ideas out of Adam Smith into his original sociology of work. When he spoke of women he was horrifying. Of course "the division of labor" begins with physiology, because one mammalian gender tends to remain with the young that it bears while the other portion hunts and gathers and kills food; because one gender develops greater muscle mass than the other. But Durkheim does not stop with muscle mass: From Durkheim we learn the startling information—compounded of the imperialist (un-Darwinian) Darwinism of Herbert Spencer and the brain research of Paul Broca and others—that women's cranial capacity is not only smaller than men's but that modern women's brains are smaller than ancient women's *because* in the modern world less work is required of women. Broca's work was seized upon by misogynists everywhere. (In an essay, Stephen Jay Gould has taken care of Broca's methodology.) "The further we look into the past," argues Durkheim, "the smaller becomes this difference between man and woman. The woman of past days was not at all the weak creature that she has become with the progress of morality." As he continues, Durkheim has women specialize in the labor of feeling—a stereotype that persists:

> It is certain that at the same time sexual labor is more and more divided. Limited first only to sexual functions, it slowly becomes extended to others. Long ago, woman retired from warfare and public affairs, and consecrated her entire life to her family. Since then, her role has become even more specialized. Today, among cultivated people, the woman leads a completely different existence from that of the man. One might say that the two great functions of the psychic life are thus dissociated, that one of the sexes takes care of the affective functions and the other of intellectual functions.

And "women must weep."

It was the social division of labor, creating industrialism under imperialism, that removed work from middle-class women while it heaped factory labor on women of the working class. In the mills of Marx's England, seven-year-olds of both sexes worked fifteen hours a day seven days a week; in dress shops women worked thirty hours without relief and died of exhaustion. In the agricultural countryside, enclosure expropriated peasants for industrial sheep farming, later replaced by deer parks. (Marx called deer "the fat cattle of the rich.") Working men and women moved to cities, where wealth was created by the mills;—and "In so far as machinery dispenses with muscular power, it becomes a means of employing laborers of slight muscular strength and those whose bodily development is incomplete, but whose limbs are all the more supple. The labor of women and children . . ." Thomas de Quincy—quoted by Marx—noted that "The numerical increase of laborers has been great, through the growing substitution of female for male, and above all, of child for adult labor. Three girls of 13, at wages of from 6 shillings to 8 shillings a week, here replaced the one man of mature age, of wages varying from 18 shillings to 45 shillings." (Compare, in progressive American capitalism, the conversion of salaried employees into part-timers without benefits.) Thus as the farms broke up—where women worked in equality with men—men lacked jobs, poor women were exploited, and their prosperous sisters languished in an idleness without purpose.

My own family achieved the middle class only recently. If Kate in New Hampshire appeared to take satisfaction in the work of kitchen and house, Augusta in Connecticut was proud of keeping the dairy's books. She and her sisters were hard-working and resourceful; having a father who worked with his hands, they were not required to languish. In the busy city they worked, clever enough to escape the factory for the office. Gussie's sister Clara labored as a secretary—shorthand, filing, typing—in the gas company, then assisted the treasurer, and lived long enough to become an executive in the same company. After Augusta married Henry, who struggled to establish and expand the Hall Dairy Company, the family joked that she was the brains and he the brawn; jokes tell the truth: She handled the office (a room in the big stucco house they lived in, with a great desk and a green leather chair), doing the payroll and handling financial matters, while Henry with his fourteen- and sixteen-hour days bought milk, bottled and delivered it.

At some point about 1920, it was revealed to Henry and Augusta that they had become members of the middle class. Gussie withdrew from bookkeeping when Brock-Hall hyphenated itself. She wore white gloves and played bridge, proper and stiff but humorous and quick to acknowledge her origins. Henry worked hard while he could, then as he grew old turned into H. F. the Chairman of the Board. It was my Uncle Arthur not my father who took to the modern world of business—employing "consultants," studying "communications." Henry built up the business, as it seemed to Henry, because he worked harder and longer than anyone else, not because of class or inheritance or education. Growing up with his own company, Henry worked with the people whose labor he hired; he prided himself that he could do the work they did. A paternal employer, he knew their families and helped them in their trouble and fired them in their drunken fecklessness and hired them back again. He intended to be fair and honorable; as the society changed around him, he turned into Management. Imagine the young boss, vigorous, with his thriving new business; he came up the hard (and only) way, delivering milk that he bottled himself, and, if an employee sicked out, working

110

twenty hours that day. Then, imagine him with thirty years added to his mustache, his stomach, and his gait, turned into H. F. who wears suits and parks a big car; he has become a state senator in Connecticut, even a minor Republican boss: When he walks through the parking lot at the dairy, the only workers he knows have white hair; younger men belong to a union and vote for Roosevelt. Henry's own sons, who went to college, sit at desks wearing white shirts and neckties, adding columns of figures.

Class in America may be a joke but it is not funny. When I was seventeen I decided I was a socialist; at prep school I subscribed to a weekly edition of *The Worker* and read it as publicly as I was able, a classic reactive pinko . . . and at home I was a boss's son: I remember crossing the dairy's parking lot walking with my father, who wore a brown suit and brown shoes and brown fedora, past young men my age in ratty clothes washing the mud from trucks. I lowered my gaze, unable to look them in the eyes.

Henry's son's wives—unlike Augusta or Clara, unlike Kate—did not work the way their mothers did. My mother becomes indignant when I say such a thing, because she worked hard and long. I exaggerate—in order to note the extraordinary difference between her life and her mother's life. My mother acquired the vote but lost a domain to rule over, nor could she provide half the labor essential to her establishment's economy. Brought up to work, and to value herself by work's accomplishment, she cooked, sewed, washed, ironed, canned, and cleaned—in the suburbs, in a six-room house, for a husband and a single child. She worked out of habit's necessity not out of necessity's habit. She washed and ironed fourteen white shirts a week; she washed and ironed sheets, pillowcases, tablecloths, and underwear. In the summer she bought bulk vegetables and fruit, she canned and made jellies and jams on a gas stove. She worked all day on these tasks, then washed, changed her clothes, and cooked supper for my father and me. She cooked breakfast for the two males also, and often lunch. No school buses in those days; school was close enough so that I walked home for lunch; and my father returned from twelve to one as we sat at the table with our ironed linen napkins.

But no matter how hard Lucy tried, her work could not matter to the suburban economy as Kate's work mattered to the farm's; in Connecticut's economy, it was cash that counted, not provision of service. In the old rural world, cash lay outside the work-center; meanwhile, the work-center was powerful to provide the necessities of warmth and nutriment—and self-esteem.

In her thirties my mother became ill with severe unexplained weight loss followed by a series of operations: gall-bladder, hysterectomy. Gradually, she recovered her vigor and acuteness. By the time my father began to die she was strong; she took tender and assiduous care of him as he wasted. He died young and she survived him—and developmental stages did not cease with widowhood at fifty-two. A year after my father's death, she developed an ulcer. She went to a surgeon looking for an operation; he said to her: "Work." As a volunteer, she worked with children at a hospital in New Haven and her health improved. Then supermarket loss-leader milk sales reduced Brock-Hall's home delivery market, the stock stopped paying dividends, the company headed toward ruin—and my mother needed a wage. She had not taught since 1927, but she took courses to bring herself up to date and in her mid-fifties entered the marketplace as a substitute teacher. She taught in Hamden schools with great success for ten years, grew more energetic

and livelier-minded as she grew older, and thrived again in a
high pride of work and accomplishment.

For Henry Moore or any ambitious work-lover there is not
only the best day but the worst. For many achievers the
worst day is depression—lethargy, discouragement, conviction of failure. Some temperaments, like Henry Moore's, are
more fortunate than others, more able to ride over a bad
patch by steady work, by playing over the pain as NFL an-
nouncers like to put it. Until sickness and death at least: Sickness and death take care of everybody. Henry suffered bad
family times late in life, estrangement from his daughter and
therefore from his grandchildren. Then a gallbladder operation almost killed him, and his short-term memory dimin-
ished catastrophically. The great worker, still wishing to rival
Michelangelo late in his eighties, sat helpless and cathetered
in his wheelchair a few years later, occasionally trying to
sketch.

It sounds like bliss: "late in his eighties." I am about to start
chemotherapy. I read the medical literature concerning my
disease and understand how poor my chances are to live
more than a few years; maybe three, but what will the third
year be like? Will there be energy enough for work? I imagine that another lesion grows rapidly, in my remaining liver.
When I panic, panic confounds itself with guilt and rage—
because Bernie Siegel, Chopra, and other visualizers tell me
that I kill myself by negative imagining, the victim guilty as
ever. Sometimes I understand that the people I love the most
believe, against their own wishes, that I have little time to
live. When we were in Connecticut Jane told me, clearly

wondering whether she should speak, that in my mother's house she kept glimpsing a man she had never seen before, a figure at the corner of her eye who vanished quickly. It was my father, she understood, who died of cancer when she was eight years old. Her notion depressed me sharply and I didn't respond. "He's just looking out for you," she suggested, but I don't think it was her only thought; the room we sleep in, in my mother's house, is the room he died in. Talking with my mother I suggested that, if she didn't return to smoking, maybe she could stay out of the hospital for, oh, maybe two whole years. She shook her head no: "One year for me," she said; "two years for you." She wasn't talking about staying out of the hospital.

When I am not working I brood and hold close to Jane. It is a dreadful absorbedness, yet I can still work much of the time, and when I work I am absorbed in work.

So often in these connections I think of Henry James who wrote a beautiful short story, "The Middle Years," that he published in *Scribner's Magazine* the year he turned fifty. (When he wrote his autobiography in old age, *The Middle Years* became the title for the second volume.) How many times have I written about this story? A novelist, "poor Dencombe," is dying in middle life—at about fifty, we might surmise. His new novel, called *The Middle Years*, arrives at the spa where he is resting, and he picks it up to read. To his pleasure he feels it is *good*—but soon he begins to weep: "he felt not so much that his last chance was going as that it was gone indeed. He had done all that he should ever do, and yet he had not done what he wanted." It comes to Dencombe that he has, in this book, finally achieved his art; now he feels "as he had never felt before that diligence *vincit omnia*." But if you do not live, you cannot be diligent. "As he turned the last leaves of his volume he murmured: 'Ah for another go!—ah for a better chance!'" He knows with bitterness that he will not have a second chance.

In the story, poor Dencombe meets an intelligent admirer of his work—and eventually he is persuaded: "A second chance—*that's* the delusion. There never was to be but one. We work in the dark—we do what we can—we give what we have. Our doubt is our passion and our passion is our task. The rest is the madness of art."

James loved to work, and like most workers he bragged about how hard he worked. Diligence *vincit omnia* was the legend he flew on his flag. In 1909, when he included "The Middle Years" in the New York Edition of his works, he spoke of "the number of times I had to do it over to make sure of it." "I scarce perhaps recall another case . . . in which my struggle to keep compression rich, if not, better still, to keep accretions compressed, betrayed for me such community with the anxious effort of some warden of the insane engaged at a critical moment in making fast a victim's straitjacket." Every morning of his grown-up life James spent writing longhand, until rheumatism in his right wrist stopped him. While he made *What Maisie Knew* (1897; "The Middle Years" belongs to the longhand phase) he learned to dictate, and for the rest of his life he wrote his fiction out loud each morning while pacing up and down, with his amanuensis seated at a typewriter.

He dictated his best work. He did not, like poor Dencombe, succumb at fifty, but wrote his best work as he aged: "The Beast in the Jungle," other late stories, and above all the three great novels: *The Wings of the Dove* (1902), *The Ambassadors* (1903), and *The Golden Bowl* (1904). Later, age and its illness interrupted work, breakdowns both mental and physical. *The American Scene* (1907) was wonderful; there were fine things in the unfinished autobiography, in the unfinished novels; there were the prefaces to his work, written for The New York Edition—but late in his life there was depression and loss; there was renewed endeavor stopped short by further failure, until he suffered his first stroke on 2 December 1915. As he fell, he later told a friend, he had the thought: "So it has come at last—The Distinguished Thing." Apparently it came wearing initial capitals, and if his life was almost over, his mind had not quite stopped its endeavor to work. After his second stroke his confusion mounted. A few days later he went back to work, as it were, riding on grooves established by sixty years of sentences in the morning. He was paralyzed on one side, but he could still speak, and the habit of two decades had been dictation. He called for his helper and worked again, making the clauses of his adult style:

> . . . we simply shift nursling of genius from one maternal breast to the other and the trick is played, the false note averted. . . . Astounding little stepchild of God's astounding young stepmother! . . . five miles off at the renewed affronts that we see coming from the great, and that we know they will accept. The fault is that they had found themselves too easily great, and the effect of that, definitely, had been, within them, the want of long provision for it.

Henry James dictated on; and on and on. The work survives the worker: Henry Moore without memory sketching in a wheelchair, Henry James on the bed of paralysis speaking a senseless syntax.

In his journals Emerson wrote, "To every reproach I know but one answer, namely, to go again to my work. 'But you neglect your relations.' Too true, then I will work the harder. 'But you have no genius.' Yes, then I will work the harder. 'But you have detached yourself from people: you must regain some positive relation.' Yes, I will work the harder."

Emerson's dutifulness is clear; his obsession is also clear, his egotism—and something like frigidity. Emerson was famous, of course; because of his lecturing, his fame was grossly public and personal, not abstract like the fame of writers known only through their books. How many dinners had he endured with fawning strangers, how many receptions? When he was old, tourists came to Concord hoping to glimpse him, the sage as a fleshy Taj Mahal. He deplored (like athletes or moviestars who cannot enter a pizza parlor) the pressing access of strangers. "Whom God hath put asunder," he said, "why should man join together?"

As ever, the work-lover detaches himself from people, not wishing to "regain some positive relation." I find myself in this respect Emersonian: Although I want to live among my children, my grandchildren, my mother, and Jane, otherwise I want to say: KEEP OUT. Is this coldness? I would rather write a letter to a friend than talk with her. Some of my friends resemble me in this regard, aging workers desperate to work; I recognize their desire with pleasure or at least with relief. On occasion we meet—these particular friends— to hug each other, to talk with excitement, and to part quickly. Loving to work has become our nature: Meister Eckhart says that the stone does its work day and night. "If it lay on the ground a thousand years, it would press downwards as much or as little as it did on the first day." Maybe

Emerson and the rest of us emulate the coldness of stone so that for a thousand years we "will work the harder."

My father, on the other hand, was a gregarious man—and it pains me to think of my father's work. He was always a victim—because he was the eldest son of a hard-working self-made man and an immigrant's hard-working daughter: Nothing he ever did was good enough. When he went to Hillhouse High School in New Haven, his parents followed the advice of friends: He took no college courses but studied mechanical drawing which he hated. Then his parents joined the middle class. When he was graduated, the smallest male in his class, they packed him off to Cushing Academy in Ashburnham, Massachusetts, for a postgraduate year that would prepare him for college. He took Greek to qualify for college when everybody else took Latin, sprinted on the track team, grew four inches, and sniffed the possibilities of happiness. His parents managed to confer some misery upon him even at Cushing; in their naivety they believed the catalog when it unconscionably claimed that students required no pocket money. Other young men and women bought five-cent sodas but my father did not have five cents.

I repeat stories I grew up on, stories that created me.

Cushing's headmaster suggested Bates College in Lewiston, Maine. When my father arrived he took a job in a diner where he worked four years for meals and pocket money. Going home to Connecticut from Maine for his vacations, he took the *State of Maine* that arrived in New Haven at dawn, whereupon he began working for the Hall Dairy all day every day (never doing anything right) until he took the train back to Lewiston, where my mother remembers him returning from Christmas or Easter vacation exhausted and ready for rest. Decades later, going over the family books, Augusta noticed that my father's four years at Bates cost less than his younger brother's first semester at Yale.

When my father was graduated from Bates in the Class of 1925 (along with Erwin Canham, who became editor of the *Christian Science Monitor* and a perennial on "Face the Nation"; along with the novelist Gladys Hasty Carroll; along with Euterpe Boukis Dukakis; along with my mother) he decided not to enter the family business. Small wonder. On the other hand, what a blow for his parents, who could not fathom his rejection; what had they struggled for, all these decades, if not to build a business for sons to carry on? Instead, my father wanted to teach; for two years at Cushing Academy he taught History (his Bates major) and English while he coached track. Bette Davis was his pupil. Meantime his father—because an eldest son decided not to join the firm—combined with Charlie Brock to form Brock-Hall. In later years, whenever the partnership caused strain, my father took the blame; if he had only come right out of college to join the Hall Dairy . . .

Teaching at Cushing he received board, room, and a thousand dollars a year. My mother taught high school in New Hampshire for wages of a similar munificence. In 1927 married women did not teach school and you didn't get married on a thousand dollars a year. Lucy and Don (I am a junior) wanted desperately to marry, to live together, to have children. In 1927 my father went back on his earlier decision and gave up teaching to work for his father; he married my mother and I was born a year later.

As far as I can tell, or remember, my father always loathed his work at the dairy. No hobby or passionate pastime suggested itself as a substitute. There was my mother, there was me, there was golf . . . Because the dairy needed someone to do figures, he did figures—and he had no mathematics and disliked arithmetic. The dairy hired someone to teach him bookkeeping; my mother, who was good at numbers, helped him—and he became facile. But even though he added long columns of figures in his head faster than anyone in the office using a Burroughs, he detested what he did. I remember him sitting at the desk night after night—shaking, pale, smoking Chesterfields, coughing—as he added numbers on 8 ½ × 11 white pads with blue lines, like the pad I write these words on.

He hated what he did and I love what I do. Opposites are never accidental. He shook his fist over my cradle, I was always told, saying, "He'll do what he wants to do"—and he stuck to it years later even when it turned out to be poetry that I wanted to do. He hated working for his father and with his younger brother—who liked business and seemed not to take it so seriously. I remember my father coming home, noon or night, weeping over "the office"—a slight, an insult, a cruel joke, the discovery of a an error.

If he had to fire someone who had stolen money from the dairy, or if he had to administer a reprimand, he came home weeping. He seemed soft to me; then softer; then softer still. With the five-day week he played eighteen holes of golf every Saturday morning, depending on the weather. He liked vacations, weekends, and eating out. Then his health fell away from him like leaves in August from a sick tree. He was pale, his hair thinned early, he woke coughing every night and quieted his cough with a Chesterfield. His hands and head shook when he was in his forties. Continually he planned to quit the dairy. He cherished a notion of the campus as a place where people were *kind* to each other—something I never noticed at the University of Michigan—and once he almost

120

arranged to teach business at Bates; but the salary was minuscule. How would he pay for my college tuition?

When he was forty-two and I was seventeen, I was clerking one Christmas at a New Haven bookstore when my mother called to say that an ambulance had taken him to the hospital after he hemorrhaged and lost a third of his blood. An ulcer had gone undetected. He recovered and took two months leave from the dairy, going to Florida with my mother and walking on the sands. He stopped smoking; he no longer woke up coughing every night; I remember him just before he went back to work, lean and tan and young-looking. But he went back to the Brock-Hall Dairy, back to insult and injury and packs of Chesterfields. When he was fifty-one exploratory surgery revealed inoperable lung cancer and he died, sixteen days after his fifty-second birthday, on a hospital bed in the guestroom on Ardmore Street.

I was twenty-seven, a fellow at Harvard, and had just published my first book of poems. He and I had become close again, affectionate, especially since the birth of my son Andrew (Donald Andrew Hall III), even though there wasn't much to talk about. I was glad for our late closeness, but I deplored his failure to thrive, which was and remains unfair of me. What chance did he have? Surely his early death, and the life that led up to it, made all the difference to me, for good and for ill. I would not let it happen to me; I would do what I wanted to do; I would work at the work I wanted to work at.

To read what I have written, you would not know that I am Christian. When I began *Life Work* I was reading the Old Testament again, loving *Genesis* (all the best stories) and hat-ing *Exodus* with the Egyptians and the Jews wreaking usual havoc on each other. When I came home from the hospital it was Corinthians and then John, an understandable change of emphasis. Meister Eckhart is my favorite heretic and now I read him again—who says that the soul desires only repose; it is the soul's nature to desire repose, as it is the stone's nature to press downwards. Yet I note that Meister Eckhart's writings are voluminous and give off energy like a radioactive pile. (The Inquisition considered him radioactive; it is astonishing how Hindu he becomes.) Meister Eckhart's energy centers on God not on Jesus—I cherish the figure of Jesus as Jack Jensen did—and he reminds me of my inability to love God as much as I love his intercessor. The cloud of unknowing remains thick over my head.

But why, when I write about my work and my day, do I not speak of the spirit? Maybe for several reasons, most of them discreditable: (1) I am afraid of ridicule; most of my friends are embarrassed by my Christianity, my Deaconhood at the South Danbury Church, and explain it away. (2) I *am* skeptical, always looking for material explanations; then at times my skepticism is overwhelmed by a spiritual light, strobe more than nightlight. (3) What I hope: Like the juggler of Our Lady, my work is my devotion. Thus, to write *Life Work* as I walk (temporarily) from the tomb is my devotion.

Jack Jensen discovered the figure of Jesus for me. Subsequently, I have read everything I could about the historical Jesus, loving Jack's history almost as much as his theology. For me, the Palestinian figure, small through the reversed telescope, continues in the present to walk two thousand years ago wearing sandals through the marketplace doing astonishing things. When he raises the dead he raises my materialist skepticism at the same time. When he withers a fig

122

tree with an impulsive petulance, I take the story as scribal interpolation. But when Jesus feeds multitudes; when he routs the money-changers; when he despairs and when he thirsts; when he tells parables and explains them; when he tells the crowd, about to stone a woman to death, that the man without sin should throw the first stone; when he eats with his friends the tax collectors; when he dies crucified— then I believe that he rises again . . .

It is all present or it is nothing.

These days I think so often about Jack—his sermons, jokes, and chatter; his long work with students and church; his slow breathing and his cold hand.

This book ends otherwise than it started. Today as I conclude a draft, it is only three months since I began. During these three months I have worked more hours on poems than I have worked on this little book: I have finished a book review and two or three short essays; I have dictated hundreds of letters; I have acquired two more grandchildren; I have helped my mother back from another heart-attack; I have lost two-thirds of a liver and nine-tenths of my complacency. I have come so close to Jane that I feel as if I had crawled into her body through her pores—and, although the occasion of this penetration has been melancholy, the comfort is luminous and redemptive. Every day she rubs my body, trunk and limbs; her hands knead my back, lift my head, pull my hair—and I feel, intensely, an interdependent fusing together of our bodies and spirits. When she lays hands on my abdomen, pausing, I know that she is praying or meditating the cancer out.

Chemotherapy begins tomorrow. When Jack Jensen

started chemotherapy, I decided to shave my head to be bald with Jack; then he spoiled my putative gesture by wearing a wig. Will I follow Jack from chemo to the memorial bench, where we prayed for him the day this book started? So often chemo means that an operation is impossible, and suggests imminent death; in my case I know it indicates no great carcinoma growing in me now—because my CEA has dropped to normal—but I understand the statistical probability that I carry a residue of malign cells: I will infuse 5FU's poison into my veins to kill cells, knowing that no one can tell me that this procedure is effective, only that it might be . . . Appetite and energy will diminish, replaced by nausea and diarrhea. What shall I *do*? Lethargy is hardly something to *do*. There are children's books I want to write; there are six long poems or sequences to work on. "The Daughters of Edward D. Boit" I can redraft three times a week; a long poem that I began fifteen years ago is two-thirds solid and intact; do I need to rewrite the other third or merely cut it out, like the lobe of a liver? The other long things are mostly done, subject to tinkering-revision, clean copy every week or two; but working them over will distract me for a long time. If I have a long time.

If little poems announce themselves I will open the door; they knock infrequently these days. But I will undertake no more long projects. I will do short stories, children's books, new short poems, maybe another essay of this length, certainly essays of a thousand words for periodicals—but no more long-term projects. Today if I begin a thought about 1995 I do not finish the thought. It is easier, and it remains pleasant, to undertake short endeavors which absorb me as much as any work can. There is only one long-term project.